Legal Research Using
WESTLAW®

The West Legal Studies Series

Your options keep growing with West Legal Studies

Each year our list continues to offer you more options for every area of the law to meet your course or on-the-job reference requirements. We now have over 140 titles from which to choose in the following areas:

Administrative Law	Family Law
Alternative Dispute Resolution	Federal Taxation
Bankruptcy	Intellectual Property
Business Organizations/Corporations	Introduction to Law
Civil Litigation and Procedure	Introduction to Paralegalism
CLA Exam Preparation	Law Office Management
Client Accounting	Law Office Procedures
Computer in the Law Office	Legal Research, Writing, and Analysis
Constitutional Law	Legal Terminology
Contract Law	Paralegal Employment
Criminal Law and Procedure	Real Estate Law
Document Preparation	Reference Materials
Environmental Law	Torts and Personal Injury Law
Ethics	Will, Trusts, and Estate Administration

You will find unparalleled, practical support

Each text is augmented by instructor and student supplements to ensure the best learning experience possible. We also offer custom publishing and other benefits such as West's Student Achievement Award. In addition, our sales representatives are ready to provide you with dependable service.

We want to hear from you

Our best contributions for improving the quality of our books and instructional materials is feedback from the people who use them. If you have a question, concern, or observation about any of our materials, or you have a product proposal or manuscript, we want to hear from you. Please contact your local representative or write us at the following address:

West Legal Studies, 3 Columbia Circle, P.O. Box 15015, Albany, NY 12212-5015

For additional information point your browser at

www.westlegalstudies.com

Legal Research Using
WESTLAW®

JUDY A. LONG, J. D.

Paralegal Coordinator
Rio Hondo College
Whittier, CA

WEST

THOMSON LEARNING™

Australia   Canada   Mexico   Singapore   'Spain   United Kingdom   United States

WEST LEGAL STUDIES

Legal Research Using Westlaw
Judy A. Long, J.D.

Business Unit Director:
Susan L. Simpfenderfer

Executive Editor:
Marlene McHugh Pratt

Acquisitions Editor:
Joan M. Gill

Editorial Assistant:
Lisa Flatley

Executive Marketing Manager:
Donna J. Lewis

Channel Manager:
Nigar Hale

Executive Production Manager:
Wendy A. Troeger

Production Editor:
Betty L. Dickson

Cover Image:

Cover Designer:

NOTICE TO THE READER

Publisher does not warrant or guarantee any of the products described herein or perform any independent analysis in connection with any of the product information contained herein. Publisher does not assume, and expressly disclaims, any obligation to obtain and include information other than that provided to it by the manufacturer.

The reader is notified that this text is an educational tool, not a practice book. Since the law is in constant change, no rule or statement of law in this book should be relied upon for any service to any client. The reader should always refer to standard legal sources for the current rule or law. If legal advice or other expert assistance is required, the services of the appropriate professional should be sought.

The Publisher makes no representation or warranties of any kind, including but not limited to, the warranties of fitness for particular purpose or merchantability, nor are any such representations implied with respect to the material set forth herein, and the publisher takes no responsibility with respect to such material. The publisher shall not be liable for any special, consequential, or exemplary damages resulting, in whole or part, from the readers' use of, or reliance upon, this material.

DEDICATION

TO DANIELLE AND JEFF

CONTENTS

PART II   WESTLAW USING WESTMATE

PREFACE

More and more law firms and corporate legal departments are subscribing to the Westlaw research service because of its easy accessibility on the Internet as well as its timeliness and accuracy. The most recent materials can be found as quickly as it takes to click the mouse on your computer. Cases are available within hours of their being published by the courts.

This textbook presents the Westlaw system in clear and concise language. The Westlaw screens described in the text are shown in figures or tables in the text so that they are easier to understand. Detailed explanations are given of the steps necessary to perform various functions.

Acknowledgments

I would like to thank my editors, Joan Gill, Lisa Flatley, and Betty Dickson for their assistance in the completion of this textbook as well as my copyeditor Maggie Jarpey. The representatives of Westlaw were very helpful in providing reference materials. I would like to particularly thank Laura Mickelson and Sally Chatelaine at Westlaw for their assistance.

Thank you also to anyone whose name was inadvertently omitted.

Judy A. Long

PART I

Westlaw on the Internet

CHAPTER 1

Introduction

The Westlaw® system is the most timely of the West systems, enabling the researcher to find pertinent information almost immediately after cases are decided by the courts. Current news, statutes, and session laws are provided. At times, however, it may be beneficial to use books—(1) for their portability and (2) for the convenience of their indices and table of contents, which enable you to find different topics and information quickly. The research materials found in West's CD-ROM library combine the capability and capacity of computers with the cost benefits of books.

The Westlaw *computer-assisted legal research (CALR)* system enables you to access current information at any time and in any place. You can search thousands of legal records and documents and read case material almost immediately after the court has handed down the decision. With access as simple as getting online and finding the Westlaw Web page, and new features such as the WIN (acronym for "Westlaw is Natural") language (described later in this book), Westlaw has become easier to use than ever before.

Once an account has been opened, you may gain access by getting online, finding the Web page (**http://www.westlaw.com**), and keying in your account number and password. In a matter of minutes you will be connected to the system. Prior to putting primary research materials (cases and statutes) online, West editors check them for accuracy and add parallel citations, editorial comments, and descriptions. The system is linked to the West books and CD-ROM library through the West key numbering system.

Twenty-four-hour access is provided to the Westlaw library of research materials. Entry is provided to approximately 15,000 different databases, representing billions of pages of information, in addition to much information that is not available in print.

THE NEW WESTLAW

A new system has been devised whereby Web technology has been combined with the more familiar book research to provide a consolidated and simple source of information. Tabs are furnished to view citations, tables of contents, statutes outlines, and other information without leaving the original document. The appearance on your screen is similar to a book's pages.

The system provides a research trail of all steps used in your current search so that you are able to navigate quickly through pages. Multiple databases can be searched simultaneously. A centralized source for key numbers assists in searches based on the West key numbering system.

WORD SEARCHES

Westlaw uses a universal feature for searching for specific words and their derivatives. If a word exists in several forms, the "!" symbol is used at the end of the word's root to find all endings of the word. For example, Westlaw may be instructed to find all forms of the word "give" by entering "giv!" into your query. In this way, you will find all occurrences of "give," "given," "giving," and all other words that begin with "giv."

Westlaw searches for the regular and irregular plural forms of the word automatically when you enter the singular form. Therefore, it is not necessary to use the "!" symbol if only the singular, plural, or possessive form of the word is required. If you wish to have Westlaw search only for the exact word and not its plural (or equivalent) form, limit the search with a "#" entered before the word itself. If you want just the plural form, enter it: for example, "Securities." Thus, "#give" will allow a search for only the word "give." Note that Westlaw will automatically find the possessive form of the word for which you are searching. If you search for "man," Westlaw will automatically find "man's" and "men's" as well. If you enter "#men," you will get "men" and "men's" but not "mens" (as in *mens rea*.)

The "*" symbol operates as if you were using it to search for material on your hard drive or a diskette. This sign represents any character of the alphabet. Using more than one sign enables a search for more than one character. Each "*" indicates one character. This symbol must be used with care, however, since some searches will reveal words not at all related to your search.

For example, using "f*ll" in your search would yield "fall," "fell," "full," and "fill." If you are searching for information for a personal injury "slip and fall" case, then, to make sure that only applicable material is found, you should write out the words "fall" and "fell" in your search query rather than using the "*" symbol.

CREATING INTERNAL WEB SITES

One major advantage of using Westlaw online is the ability to set up internal Web sites to link content. Most legal offices have their own *intranets* that link members of the firm via their computers. Individuals in the office may conduct their research using Westlaw, file it in the firm's research files on their computer, and link the research so that it goes directly to a page on

http://www.westlaw.com.

If someone else in the office is interested in the topic of that particular research, he or she may click the hyperlink and find the correct page.

By the use of *WestCiteLink*, a hyperlink can be created that links the citations in a document and the text of the case on Westlaw. Thus, if another member of the firm is conducting research into a given topic, that person may follow the existing link to the citations and cases.

# KEYCITE

You are probably familiar with the system for updating cases and statutes in books. You must look through several citators to determine whether the case or statute you wish to utilize has been overruled or amended before using it in your current document. Often several books have to be checked for the appropriate citation. This process may take several hours if many cases or statutes are being cited.

With the use of KeyCite, you can obtain this information by a click of the mouse on your computer. Information that might take several hours using books is acquired in minutes. The details of the case history are provided online within a few hours of the time the court opinion is received by West. Unreported cases are also available.

PRIMARY SOURCES

Primary sources—that is, binding authority, including laws, case decisions, administrative regulations, and other similar sources of law—are available on Westlaw for all 50 states and the District of Columbia. It is a relatively simple process to find cases from any of these places on any subject by doing a "key word search" with all the words that must be present in the case. Within seconds the citations for the most recent cases are given on the screen. You merely click on the case in which you are interested, and that case appears on your screen.

Opinions of the United States Supreme Court are available within an hour of the time they are released by the court. The special "highlights" databases provide significant new court opinions on given topics on a daily basis.

Statutes and administrative codes from the states as well as the federal system are available under the codes for the individual states and the United States codes.

SECONDARY SOURCES

Secondary sources are persuasive authority, including legal comments, annotations, articles in legal periodicals or law reviews, and legal encyclopedias. Almost any secondary source available in a library can be found on Westlaw. More than 10,000 databases can be accessed. Among these are legal newspapers, public records, international newspapers, general-interest magazines and journals, newsletters and trade publications on many topics, and press releases. Practice area materials are available in several different specialties, such as administrative law, bankruptcy, business organizations, government, family law, and many more. General texts and periodicals can be found, as well as treatises, practice guides, journals, and law reviews. The *West Legal Directory* provides information about attorneys in the United States and in some foreign countries.

WESTLAW VIA THE WEB OR WESTMATE

The easiest method of accessing Westlaw may be through your Internet browser via the World Wide Web by using the Westlaw home page (**http://www.westlaw.com**). You must first obtain an account from West, along with a password. You can then go to the Web page, key in your account number and password, and you will be online with Westlaw.

As an alternative, you may obtain an account that includes Westmate software and connect to the database directly via your modem. You will need to load the software onto your computer and make use of special commands provided in your subscription materials, as well as in Chapters 10 and 11 of this text. Part I of this book will focus on the use of Westlaw via the World Wide Web. Part II includes some discussion on accessing Westlaw using Westmate software for Windows. However, the instructions for the use of Westlaw given in Part I apply also to using Westmate. Therefore, the reader using Westmate should read Part I thoroughly before reading Part II, which provides a brief discussion of the unique features of Westmate.

Information about either of these two systems may be obtained through West's Customer Service Department at 1-800-Westlaw or 1-800-937-8529. Ordering and pricing information is available from West Sales Support at 1-800-328-9352.

REVIEW QUESTIONS

1. Define primary and secondary sources.
2. What two methods are available for gaining access to Westlaw?
3. Explain how to gain access to Westlaw using both methods described in Review Question 2.

CHAPTER 2

Getting Online with Westlaw

In order to go immediately to Westlaw, perform the following steps on your computer:

1. Get online with your Web browser, either Netscape Navigator 3.0 or higher, or Microsoft Explorer 3.0 or higher.

2. In the "Go to" section of the browser page, key in the following address and hit "Enter."

http://www.westlaw.com

3. Go to the "Sign on to westlaw.com" dialog box.

4. Type in your Westlaw password in the "Password" box and your Client Identifier in the "Client ID" box.

5. Click the "Sign on" button.

6. The "Welcome to New Westlaw.com" page will appear (see Figure 2-1, page 10), and you are ready to start your research session.

If you choose to save your Westlaw password so that you don't have to key it each time you sign on, select the option on the sign-on screen that says "Save this password." Note that anyone who uses your Web browser will be able to sign on to Westlaw with your saved password if you select this option. Therefore, it is advisable to use the option only in those cases where access to your computer is password-protected. If you wish to use the secure sign-on site feature instead, click this option so that your password will be encrypted as it is sent through the Internet.

Suppose that you do not wish to go directly to this page. In that case, you may use the home page for law schools by substituting the following address for the one used in Step 2:

http://lawschool.westlaw.com

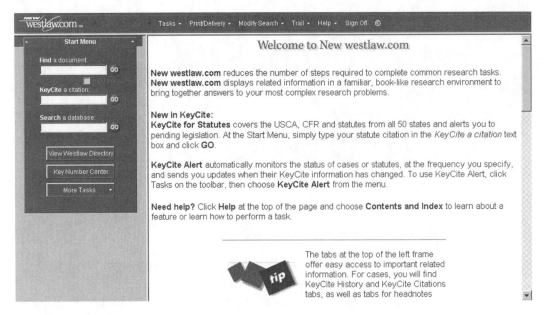

FIGURE 2-1   Westlaw Welcome Page

This will enable you to access the home page for law schools, where you will also find KeyCite, West's Educational network (TWEN), the West Legal Directory, and Westlaw.

BEGINNING YOUR RESEARCH SESSION

Figure 2-1 represents the first page you will see upon signing on to Westlaw. On the left side of the screen, you will see the "Start Menu" frame with four different choices:

1. *Find a document.* The first box enables you to find a document if you have the citation. Type the citation in the box and click the "Go" button. You will be taken to the document.

2. *Keycite a citation.* This box enables you to check a citation for accuracy or updating. Again, simply enter the citation.

3. *Search a database.* If you know the identifier for the database you wish to access, type it in this box and click the "Go" button. You will be taken to the appropriate database. Note that a list of databases available on

Westlaw is provided with subscription materials. Most of the identifiers are relatively easy to remember. Among the most common are

Name of Item	Database Identifier
Federal case law	ALLFEDS
State case law (all states)	ALLSTATES
California cases	CA-CS
New York cases	NY-CS
Virginia Statutes Annotated	VA-ST-ANN
Harvard Law Review	HVLR
All cases	ALLCASES
Wall Street Journal	WSJ

The left side of the page has a button for the *Westlaw Directory* to access the Main Directory List of databases. This feature is useful if you are not certain which database to access or if you know the name of the database but do not know its identifier. You can browse through sections of the directory by clicking on the main icon for that directory. By clicking on the icon of the database you wish to view, you will descend through various sections of the database directories.

When browsing through the directory, notice the icon (**i**) to the left of the name. Clicking on this icon will give you information about what is included in that database. The identifier for the particular database is found in the right column of the list. The Westlaw Directory page is shown in Figure 2-2 on page 12.

SEARCHING FOR A DATABASE

When you cannot find a database, use the search feature as follows:

1. On the left side of the Westlaw Directory page click the topic of your database under "Database Directory."
2. You will see a text box on the right side that enables you to search for a database using Natural Language. Type a description of the database or the type of material in which you are interested.
3. Click the "Search" button.

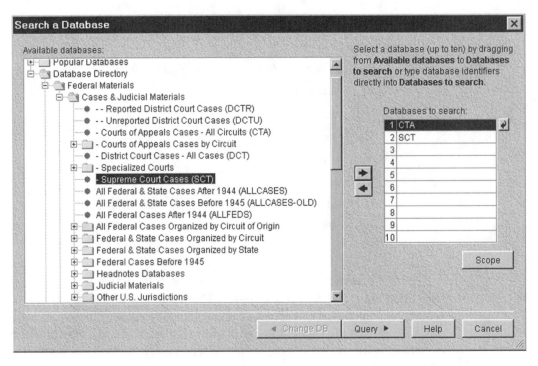

FIGURE 2-2 Westlaw Database Directory

4. Once you have completed your search, click the "View result" button if you are not using the latest version of Westlaw. If you are using **web2.westlaw.com** you will see a list in the left frame and "Document 1" in the right frame of your screen. You can then scroll through the left frame.

5. You will see a list of databases that correspond to your description. Click on the database identifier in which you are interested, or, if you would like a description of the database, click the retrieval number of that database.

6. For a more detailed description of the database, click on the Scope icon (I) or the Scope option on the left side of the Search page.

7. To leave this function, click your browser's "Back" button.

Note that the procedures may be slightly different depending on the version of Westlaw you are using.

Figure 2-2 is the Main Directory List for the Database Directory. Click the icon in front of the material if you wish to view the sections included in that particular directory. When you find the section in which you are interested, double-click on the name or identifier.

REVIEW QUESTIONS

1. Explain the steps to gain access to Westlaw once you have signed on with your Web browser.
2. What are the advantages and disadvantages of saving your West password?
3. What is the law school page where you can gain access to the *West Legal Directory*?
4. How would you find this case: *United States v. Clark,* Volume 41 of *United States Reports* at page 342?
5. How would you find the database for cases in your state? Find a recent case on consumer fraud in home improvement.

CHAPTER 3

Finding Documents

I f you are looking for a document and know either its citation or its title, you do not have to access a database to find the material. The methods of retrieval are described in this chapter.

FINDING A DOCUMENT BY CITATION

Go back to the home page that says "Welcome to New Westlaw.com." Complete the following steps for finding a document by its citation number:

1. On the left side you will see a text box that says "Find a Document."
2. Type the citation for your document in the text box (for example, **Smith v. Jones, 24 U.S. 555**).
3. Click "Go."

If you are not at the Welcome page but are elsewhere in the Westlaw system, follow these steps:

1. Locate the drop-down list at the top of the page.
2. Select "Find a document."
3. Click "Go."
4. When the "Find a document" page appears (Figure 3-1, page 16), type the citation in the "Enter a citation" box on the left side of the screen. After you have found one document, you can find others by simply typing a new cite in the box and clicking "Go."

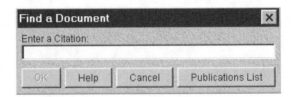

FIGURE 3-1 "Find" Page

In most cases, punctuation and spacing are optional. However, your citation request must use the proper format for citations. Some examples of "Find" requests follow:

Type of Document	*Citation Number Sample*
U.S. Code Annotated	22 USCA s 333 (or 22 usca s 333)
Federal Case	55 F2D 2222 (or 55 f2d 2222)

DOCUMENTS AVAILABLE USING "FIND"

Many publications are accessible by using the "Find" function. Notice the "Publications list" on the right side of the "Find" page. Click on this list to see all publications available using find. The abbreviations for these documents will also be included.

FINDING A DOCUMENT BY ITS TITLE

Suppose you have the name of a document but do not know the citation number. You can restrict your search by using the title field and the name of your document. First you must access the appropriate database. For example, if you were seeking the case of *Miller v. California* and you knew it was a United States Supreme Court case, you would search the database for the Supreme Court (SCT). Type the following inquiry in the Terms & Connectors text box, and click "Search":

ti(miller & california)

In order to see the case, click the "View result" field. A sample search page for finding a document by its title is shown in Figure 3-2.

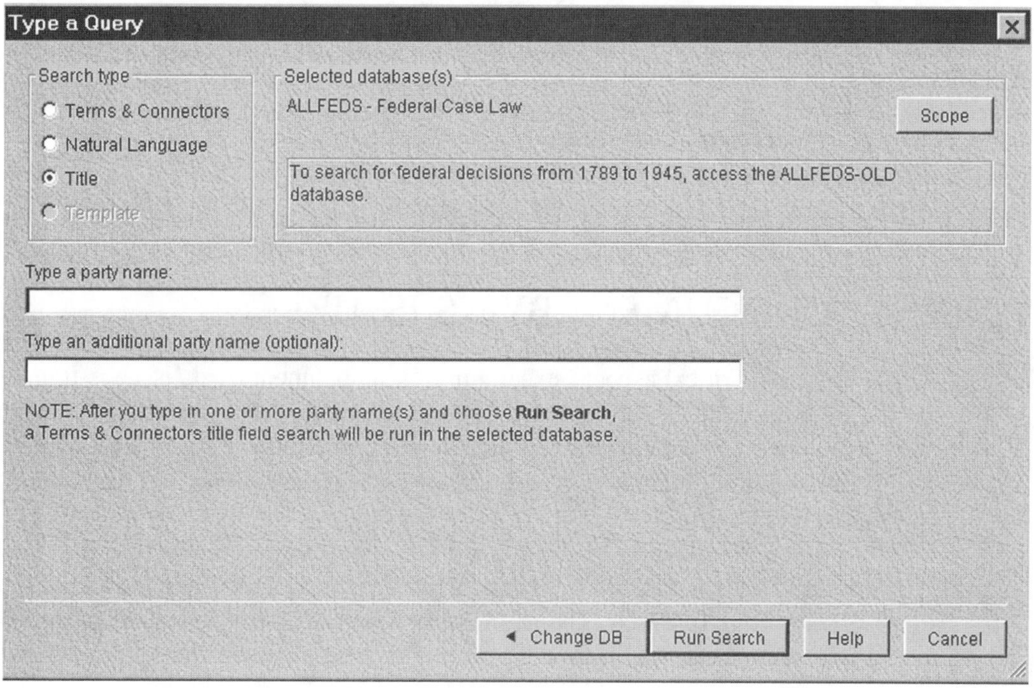

FIGURE 3-2 Searching by Title

To perform a search by title, you must precede the name of the document by the term **"ti."** Instead of using "v." in a case name, you must use **"&."** Capitalization is not required, and general terms such as plaintiff, defendant, company, or corporation should be excluded. Unique terms from the title should be used if the case name is a long one. For example, if you were searching for a case called *Jonathan Danielli Enterprises, Inc. v. Michael Jeffries Manufacturing Company, Inc.,* you would use the following search term:

ti(Danielli & Jeffries)

To find a case where both the plaintiff and the defendant have the same name, you must use the "+p" connector. For example, to find the California case of *Marvin v. Marvin,* type the following query:

ti(marvin +p marvin)

While case name titles use the names of the parties, law reviews or other periodicals use the exact title of the article itself. For example, to find an article entitled "Surrogate Parenting" in the *Harvard Law Review,* search by title in the database for *Harvard Law Review* with the following query:

   ti(surrogate parenting)

FINDING A DOCUMENT BY ITS ISSUE

The most critical aspect of searching for a document by its issue is framing the issue itself. You must also determine exactly what types of documents you wish to retrieve. Often other resources are valuable for this preliminary investigation, including digests, treatises, legal encyclopedias, periodicals, and hornbooks.

Once you have read these materials, you may be ready to frame your issue. Make a list of all pertinent terminology, facts, and concepts that define your research. Using these key words, write an issue in one or two sentences. For instance, you might have an issue that states the following:

May an owner of real property transfer ownership and still maintain a homestead?

After you have written the issue, determine what other words have the same meaning and might be used in any documents you are searching. For instance, in our example issue, "real property" can also be referred to as "real estate" or "land."

Next you must decide what types of documents you wish to retrieve as well as where you can find them. Ask yourself the following questions:

1. What type of case do I have?
2. In what jurisdiction is the case being heard?

Your list of databases should be consulted to determine the appropriate choices. For instance, if you wish to search all jurisdictions, then you should use the ALLCASES database (see Figure 3-3a). However, if you are searching only New York cases, you should use the New York cases' database. A checklist has been provided in Figure 3-3b on page 20 to assist in the search steps.

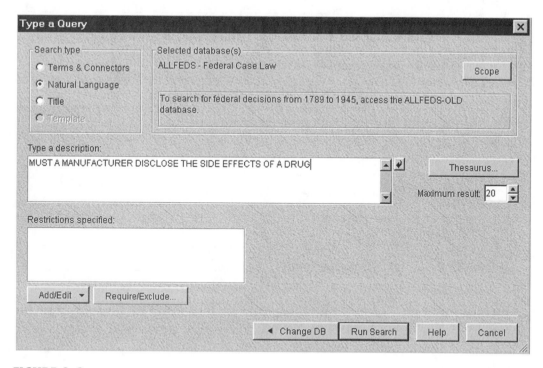

FIGURE 3-3a

Now that you have all of the preliminary information, you are ready to begin your search using the Natural Language feature called WIN, or "Westlaw Is Natural." The steps to follow are

1. Access the appropriate database.
2. Click "Natural Language" in the left frame of the page.
3. Type the description of your issue in the box called "Type a Description."
4. A list of the twenty documents most closely matching your query appears. Click the hyperlink citation in each case in order to see these documents.

On the left side of the page, you will see the citations for the twenty documents. Their text appears on the right side of the page, the ones with the most matches appearing first. A sample page that resulted from a Natural Language search is shown in Figure 3-4 on page 21.

1. **Preliminary research documents**

    A. Encyclopedia

    B. Hornbook

    C. Treatise

    D. Other

2. **Frame the issue**

    Issue statement: _____

    A. All key words _____

    B. Thesaurus Terms _____

3. **What documents do I want?** _____
    _____

4. **Natural language or terms and connectors?** _____
    _____

5. **List of databases to search:**

    Federal _____

    All states _____

    State of California only _____

    Others: _____   _____
            _____   _____
            _____   _____

6. **Have I found all relevant materials?** _____
    _____

7. **Do I want to expand my search to other databases or sources?** _____
    _____

FIGURE 3-3b Checklist for Searching by Issue

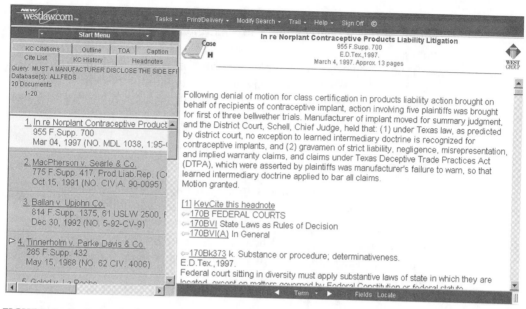

FIGURE 3-4 Sample Search Result—Natural Language

REFINING TOOLS

Several devices are available on Westlaw to further refine your search. These tools help to make your search easier as well as more comprehensive.

Searching for Multi-Word Phrases

If you wish to have certain phrases appear in your description of the issue and in the search results, you may enclose them in quotation marks. For instance, to have the phrase "res ipsa loquitur" appear in your search result, type it in quotation marks in your issue phrase.

Using Online Thesaurus to Refine Search

You may wish to have related concepts added to your description. Westlaw provides an online thesaurus to assist in this endeavor. Once you have typed your issue statement into the text box, click "Thesaurus." Look through the "Terms in the Description" list, and select that term for which you want to use related concepts. Click "View Related Terms." Select the concept you wish to add to your issue, and click "Add Term(s) to Description." Once you complete this process, click "Go" and then the "Search" button to begin your search.

If you cannot find the related term for which you are searching in the Westlaw thesaurus, you may add it by typing the description in parentheses immediately following the concept to which it relates in your issue statement.

Using Control Concepts

You can further refine your search by using Control Concepts, which allows you to specify terms that must appear in every document in your result. Type your explanation in the "Natural Language Description" box and click "Control Concepts." When the Concepts list appears on the right side of the page, select the concept you wish to appear in every document, and click "Go."

TERMS & CONNECTORS SEARCHES

In many cases, you may not want to use the Natural Language search feature of Westlaw but instead conduct a search using "Terms & Connectors" in the following manner:

1. Formulate all of the terms you wish to use in your search. Alternatives are discussed under "Appropriate Terminology" in this chapter.

2. Determine the specific connectors you wish to use between the search terms.

3. Access the database you need for this particular search.

4. Select the "Terms & Connectors" search method.

5. Enter your issue.

APPROPRIATE TERMINOLOGY

A search using the "Terms & Connectors" method is somewhat different from a "Natural Language" search. Consider the following when writing your issue, some of which points also apply to a Natural Language search:

1. *Alternative words*—Use synonyms and antonyms, variations of terms. For example, if your search involved the word "litigation," you would also wish to use the term "lawsuit." You can check the Westlaw thesaurus for alternative terms to use in your query.

2. *Common words*—Avoid common words. Examples include *it, the, they, you,* and *I.* If you enter a too-common term, you will receive a message that your terms are too common to be searched. An exception is the use of a hyphenated term as either the first or last word of your query.

3. *Plurals/possessives*—Westlaw will automatically retrieve all plural forms of words used in your issue. However, it will not retrieve the singular form if you enter the plural. The same holds true for the use of possessive terms. If you enter the word without the possessive, Westlaw will retrieve both the nonpossessive and possessive forms of the word. However, if you enter only the possessive form, the nonpossessive form will not be retrieved.

4. *Acronyms*—In order to retrieve all forms of the acronym, enter the name with periods and no spaces, and spell out the words that make up the acronym as well. For example, to find information about General Motors Corporation, you would use the following terms in your search:

"GM" or "GMC"

"General Motors" or "General Motors Corporation"

5. *Root Expanders*—In order to retrieve all forms of a word, you must use the "!" root expander at the end of the word root, which is not required in WIN. In other words, if you wish to find all forms of the word "sleep," you would enter the following term:

"sleep!"

and would retrieve the following variations of the word:

sleeping

sleeps

sleeper

6. *Asterisk*—The asterisk is used to take the place of a variable character. Use as many asterisks as you wish to show that number of variable characters. For example, using

dr*nk

will yield *drink, drank,* or *drunk.*

7. *Connectors*—Rules for using connectors follow:

    a. Either/or: A space between words indicates at least one of the terms must appear in the document.

    b. All terms (&): The & sign retrieves documents containing two or more of the search terms; however, they may be contained anywhere in the document.

    c. Same sentence (/s) or paragraph (/p): Using the /p connector requires that the same terms must appear in the same paragraph. Using the /s requires that the same terms must appear in the same sentence.

    d. Certain number of words (/n): Using a numerical connector will require that the same terms must appear within that number of words (n represents a number).

    e. Terms in quotation marks (" "): Terms must appear in the same order as they appear within the quotation marks.

    f. Excluding terms with %: Search terms following the % symbol should be excluded from the search.

Some examples of the preceding rules follow:

- **"Attorney malpractice doctor"** will retrieve any documents that contain any one of those terms.
- **"Attorney & malpractice & doctor"** will retrieve documents containing all three terms anywhere in the document.
- **"Attorney /p malpractice /p doctor"** will retrieve documents containing all three terms within the same paragraph.
- **"Attorney /s malpractice /s doctor"** will retrieve documents containing all three terms within the same sentence.
- **"Attorney /5 malpractice"** will retrieve documents containing the word "attorney" within five words of the word "malpractice."

Although the Terms & Connectors search may appear to be more difficult and cumbersome than the Natural Language search, there will often be situations where the use of the code terms applicable in this type of search are more beneficial for finding appropriate documents for your issue statement. Additional terms will allow you to restrict your search by date or by court.

FINDING DOCUMENTS BY DATE

If you are searching for cases, statutes, or articles published on a certain date or within a range of dates, go to the Terms & Connectors search page (Figure 3-5), and perform the following steps:

1. Click "Field Restrictions" on the Terms & Connectors search page.
2. Choose "Data DA" from the list.
3. Type the date within parentheses.
4. Click "Go." (Be sure your cursor is at the end of the query.)

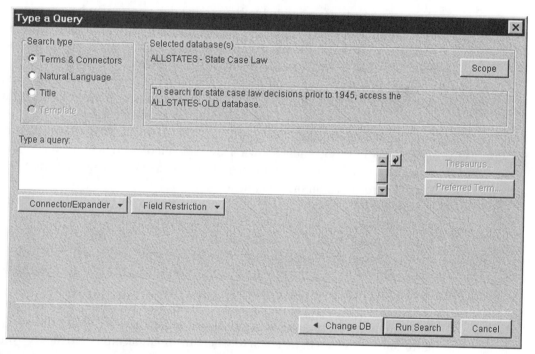

FIGURE 3.5 Terms & Connectors Search Page

An alternative method for finding a document by date follows:

1. Type **"da"** in the Terms & Connectors query text box
2. Type the date or date range in parentheses, being sure to type the year with four digits, e.g., 1988.

Some acceptable formats for dates follow:

da 9-6-1977	for documents dated September 6, 1977
da (bef 1977)	for documents before 1977
da (bef 10-10-2000)	for documents before October 10, 2000
da (aft 1979 and bef 1985)	for documents 1980–1984

SURVEYING RETRIEVED DOCUMENTS

Various methods are provided to browse the documents you have retrieved to determine if they are applicable to your original issue statement. Westlaw furnishes procedures for surveying retrieved documents, changing the display, and moving between documents on your screen.

Note the search result page on the display in Figure 3-6. On the left side, you will see a list of citations applicable to your issue statement. The right side shows the actual text of the documents from the citations.

Using the scroll bar on the right side of the screen enables you to read the entire text of the document shown. However, a more efficient method of determining whether the document is relevant to your issue is to use the "Term" arrows within the document itself.

Note the terms in your issue statement within the document. They will be shown in bold type with arrows before and after the term. If you wish to see the next page containing your search terms, click the right arrow in the "Term" box in the upper-right portion of the page, and it will take you to the next page, where the requirements of your query were met if you have used a Terms & Connectors search.

For example, clicking on "design & defect & automobile" will take you to where any of these words occur. If you search for **"design /5 defect /p automobile,"** you will be taken to where the relationship is satisfied. If you have used a Natural Language search, clicking the arrow will move you to the first of up to five portions of the document that most closely matches your description.

If you wish to find the portion of the document that most closely matches your Natural Language description, click the "Best" arrow in the upper-right portion of the screen. You will be able to move to the five closest matches to your issue description. A quick reference guide for browsing documents is shown in Figure 3-7.

To revise your search, click **Modify Search** on the toolbar and choose **Edit Query.**

Use the
Information
Tabs to view
related
information
such as KeyCite
history and
citations, case
headnotes or
the table of
contents for
statutes.

Number of
documents
in result.

Document citation.

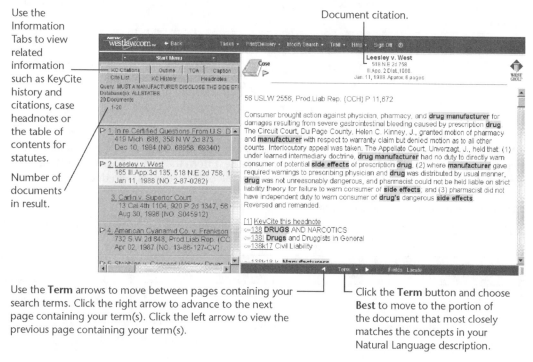

Use the **Term** arrows to move between pages containing your
search terms. Click the right arrow to advance to the next
page containing your term(s). Click the left arrow to view the
previous page containing your term(s).

Click the **Term** button and choose
Best to move to the portion of
the document that most closely
matches the concepts in your
Natural Language description.

FIGURE 3-6 Search Result Page

Browsing Within a Document	
If you want to move	**Then**
Line by line	Click the down scroll arrow.
By scrolling	Position your cursor on the down scroll arrow and hold down the mouse button.
To an approximate page	Drag the scroll box along the scroll bar to the page's approximate position.
To the next occurrence of your search terms	Click the **Term** arrow at the bottom of the right frame.

FIGURE 3-7 Quick Reference Guide to Browsing Documents

Browsing Within a Document	
If you want to move	**Then**
To terms not necessarily included in your search	Click the **Locate** button at the bottom of the right frame. In the Locate Editor dialog box, type the terms you want to locate (formulated as a Terms and Connectors query) and click **Locate**. Use the **Term** arrows to move between pages containing your Locate terms.
To the part of the document that most closely matches your Natural Language description	Click **Term** at the bottom of the right frame then choose **Best** from the menu. Click the **Best** arrows to view the best portion of each document.
From a case headnote to the corresponding text in the opinion	Click the headnote number.

Moving Between Documents	
If you want to view	**Then**
The next document, or a specific document in your search result	From the citations list in the left frame, click the document's retrieval number or title.
The previous or next group of documents in your search result	Click the arrow on the Cite List tab.
The next document in sequence even though it was not retrieved by your search or Find request (e.g., the next sequential statute)	Click the **Docs In Seq** button at the bottom of the right frame. To cancel, click the **Cancel Docs in Seq** button.
A cited document	Click the hypertext link.
The table of contents (for a statute, regulation or rule)	Click the **TOC** tab.
Update information (for a statute, regulation or rule)	Click the **KC History** tab.

FIGURE 3-7 (*continued*)

HYPERTEXT LINKS

You may already be familiar with using *hypertext links* to move from one document to another. These links are provided within your retrieved documents to enable you to immediately go to case law, law review articles, headnotes, state statutes, court rules, and other information. If you see an underlined name in a different color in your document, click on it to go to the material referenced in the hyperlink.

For instance, if you are reading the case headnotes, you will notice that each numbered headnote is a hypertext link. Clicking on the link will take you to the portion of the court decision where that particular headnote is discussed.

USING LOCATE FUNCTION

Note the drop-down list at the top of your screen. Select "Locate" from the list, and click either "Go" or "Locate" depending on your version of Westlaw. You should then formulate a Locate request as you would a Terms & Connectors search to find the portions of the document that contain the words in your Locate query. Use the Term arrows to move between the pages that contain your Locate terms. You can exit the Locate search by selecting "Cancel Locate" from the drop-down list in the left frame and clicking "Go."

FINDING PUBLIC RECORDS

Millions of public records may be found on Westlaw from across the United States if your subscription includes this service. Through a system of "fill-in-the-blank" templates, you can access business and corporate filings, UCC filings, liens, judgments, lawsuits, and bankruptcy records. The *People Finder* enables you to find people by their name and by individual state. Through the *Asset Locator,* you can find real property assessors' records by state, real property transfers, foreclosures, refinances, aircraft records, watercraft records, and stock locator records.

All of this information is accessible via the Westlaw home page. Listed here are some of the records available, along with their database identifications:

Business and Corporate Filings	*Database*
Corporate and limited partnership records	CORP-ALL
Corporate and limited partnership records by state* (does not include NJ and DE)	XX-CORP
Business Finder records—U.S.	BUSFIND-US
Business Finder records by state*	XX-BUSFIND
UCC Filings, Liens, and Judgments	
Combined UCC filings, liens, civil judgment filings	ULJ-ALL
By state*	XX-ULJ
Lien records by state*	XX-LJ
People Finder	
People Finder—Track by name	PEOPLE-NAME
People Tracker by Name—Individual States*	XX-PEOPLE
Bankruptcy Records	
Combined records	BKR-ALL
Combined records by state*	XX-BKR
Lawsuit Records	
Combined records	LS-ALL
Combined records by state*	XX-LS
Asset Locator	
Real property assessor's records	RPA-ALL
Real property assessor's records by state*	XX-RPA

*XX is the state's postal abbreviation

Asset Locator

Real property asset transfers	RPT-ALL
Real property asset transfers by state*	XX-RPT
Real property foreclosures	RPF-ALL
Real property foreclosures by state*	XX-RPF

A full listing of all public records accessible from Westlaw may be found in the *Westlaw Database Directory.*

Corporate law offices would find the business and corporate filings extremely valuable in those cases where it is necessary to obtain financial information about a corporate adverse party in a lawsuit. The People Finder may prove valuable in searching for those elusive individuals who are avoiding service or the payment of a judgment against them. The Asset Locator may prove useful in finding assets to attach for those opposing parties who owe the client money damages from an adverse judgment.

REVIEW QUESTIONS

1. Find the United States Supreme Court case of *Miller v. California* that relates to the Vietnam War. What is its citation?

2. List three law review articles related to cohabitation agreements or property in your state.

3. Find a case in your state dealing with whether a prior owner may maintain a homestead on a residence that has been sold to a family member. List its citation.

4. Frame an issue for the search on homesteads in Review Question 3 using the Natural Language feature.

5. How could you be certain that "res ipsa loquitur" would appear in your search result?

6. Why and when would you use an asterisk in your search?

7. List the possible connectors, and explain what each one means.

8. What is the database identification for finding corporate records in your state?

CHAPTER 4

Printing and Downloading

Westlaw enables you to print or download documents on a printer attached to your computer, on a fax machine, or as an attachment to e-mail. Once downloaded, the document can be saved in your word processor.

WL PRINT/DOWNLOAD BUTTON

Click on the "WL Print/Download" button to display the print/download page (Figure 4-1, page 34). Various options appear on the left side of the page. You may choose to print the current document, selected documents, all documents, or a list of citations. On the right side of the page, you may choose to print or download the complete result of your search ("Full text") only all term mode or all best mode pages, or the first page of the document including the West abstract (if this is available.) You must also choose your destination option from the right side of the page, including

1. Stand-alone printer
2. Fax machine
3. E-mail
4. Download

DESTINATIONS

Choosing the options for "Attached Printer" or "Stand Alone Printer" under "Destination" on the left side of the Print/Delivery page will send your

WestMate 7.2: To print or download documents, choose **Print/Delivery** from the File menu and select a delivery destination.

Select a print option for your document. For example, in a Natural Language search result, select **Best mode pages** to print the pages containing the portion of the document most closely matching the concepts in your description.

Print your document, the current Information Tab or the KeyCite information for the document.

Print multiple documents or list items by selecting a range.

Select **Highlight search terms** to print search terms from your document in bold type.

Select where to deliver your documents.

Select **Print case status flags** to print KeyCite status flags that are displayed in your documents.

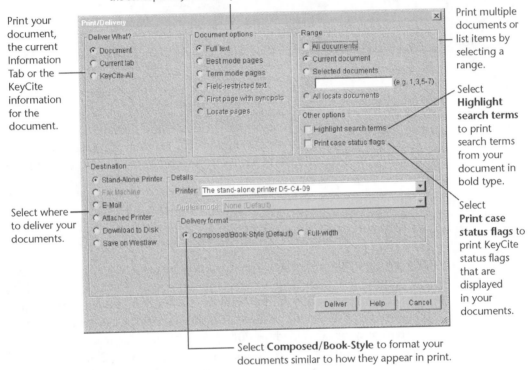

Select **Composed/Book-Style** to format your documents similar to how they appear in print.

FIGURE 4-1   Print/Download Page

request to the designated printer. If you choose "Fax Machine" as a destination, you will have the opportunity to designate the fax telephone number, the name of the individual or firm to whom the material is being faxed, your name, and the subject matter.

Choosing "E-mail" enables you to send the material to someone via e-mail. Just key in the e-mail address of the recipient.

If you choose the "Download to Disk" option, you must specify the disk to which the item should be sent. You have the option of choosing a particular word processor format. You may also select a separate option to highlight your search terms in the materials being downloaded.

DOWNLOAD AND PRINTING FORMATS

A number of different options are available to you for downloading or printing documents from Westlaw as shown in Figure 4-2. These options will now be explained in detail.

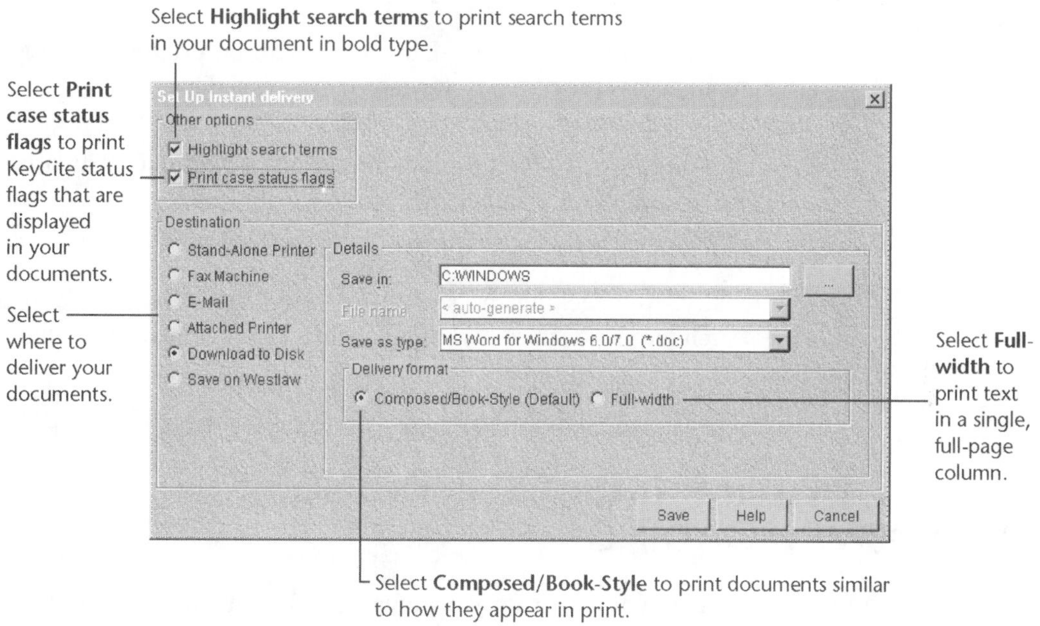

Select **Highlight search terms** to print search terms in your document in bold type.

Select **Print case status flags** to print KeyCite status flags that are displayed in your documents.

Select where to deliver your documents.

Select **Full-width** to print text in a single, full-page column.

Set Up Instant delivery

Other options
☑ Highlight search terms
☑ Print case status flags

Destination
○ Stand-Alone Printer
○ Fax Machine
○ E-Mail
○ Attached Printer
● Download to Disk
○ Save on Westlaw

Details
Save in: C:\WINDOWS
File name: < auto-generate >
Save as type: MS Word for Windows 6.0/7.0 (*.doc)

Delivery format
● Composed/Book-Style (Default)   ○ Full-width

Save   Help   Cancel

Select **Composed/Book-Style** to print documents similar to how they appear in print.

FIGURE 4-2   Downloading and Printing Formats

DOWNLOADING TO WORD PROCESSOR

Three different word processor options are available in Westlaw for downloading purposes:

1. Word for Windows (at least 6.0)
2. Wordperfect for Windows (at least 5.1)
3. PDF (Note that you must download Adobe Acrobat Reader to use this format. On the left side of the screen, choose "Get Acrobat Reader" to download this option free.)

The word processor option may be chosen from the drop-down list on the right side of your screen.

PRINTING FORMATS

Note the list of printing formats available on the right side of the screen below the drop-down list for the word processor. You must select the format you wish to use by clicking in the appropriate circle. One of the following formats may be chosen:

1. *Composed/Single Column*—Documents will be printed in a single column across the page, as they appear in print. This option is available for statutes and law review articles.

2. *Composed/Dual-Column*—Documents will be printed in two columns, as they appear in a West reporter.

3. *Full Width*—Documents will be printed in a single, full-page format.

Additionally, by checking the square for "Highlight Terms," you can have the search terms you used highlighted when the document is printed or downloaded.

SETTING UP DEFAULTS FOR PRINTING AND DOWNLOADING

Westlaw enables you to set up your own defaults for printing and downloading. You have the option of choosing the printer to which print requests are delivered, the e-mail address for print requests, and the fax machine number for print requests. To begin this process, you must choose "Options" from the drop-down list at the top of the page. Then, click on "WL Print/Download" with your mouse in order to change your default options as follows:

1. *Printer*—Select the printer to which you wish your print requests to be delivered.

2. *E-mail*—Type in the e-mail address to which you wish your print requests to be delivered. It may be your own address for temporarily storing print requests.

3. *Fax machine*—Select one of the available fax machines or add the information for your fax machine. This machine will show as the default on your Print/Download page. You must then choose either "Composed/Book-Style," for documents to be printed as they are in

books in two columns, or "Full-width" for documents to be printed the complete width of the page.

You may then choose "Save All" on the bottom right side of the page to save all of your new default settings. These settings will remain your default settings until and unless you go through the process again to make further changes.

PRINTING OFFLINE

In order to save connection charges, it may be advantageous to find the document you need and then print it offline. To perform this task, you may type

pr<enter>

or choose the appropriate commands from the pull-down menus or buttons. You will then see the menu on your screen for offline printing and downloading. Several commands may be used at this point, but only those that will work on your own terminal will be displayed. Some of the commands you may type follow:

Commands	*What it Does*
D	All pages in the current document are displayed.
L	Only the last page in the current document will print.
P#	Selected pages in the current document will print; type in the appropriate page numbers where "#" appears.
D#	All pages of the documents you select will print.
F#	If this option is available on your terminal, the first page of the documents you select will print; this will include the synopsis of the case by West.
L#	A list of citations for documents selected will print.
AD	All pages of all documents will print.

See the *WESTLAW Desktop Command Reference* for further commands.

Once you have typed in the command, you will see a summary of your commands with a list of destinations displayed. If the default destination is not the same one to which you want the listed items sent, then you can type in the appropriate command for the required destination. Some samples follow:

DLD	The indicated items will be downloaded to a diskette.
STP	The items listed will be sent to your stand-alone printer and held.
NOW	The items listed will be sent to your stand-alone printer and printed immediately.
EML	The designated items will be sent to a specific e-mail address that you indicate.

The confirmation screen will display your commands, at which point you can confirm the destination by hitting "**Enter**" or change the request by typing "**opd**" and indicating a new entry.

COMMAND STACKING

An option you can use to save a considerable amount of time is *command stacking* (available with Westmate only), which allows you to enter several commands at the same time. This way you can avoid going from screen to screen when this effort is not required. The commands are separated by semicolons to take you from one item to the last one without having to go to the screens in between. For instance, suppose you wish to retrieve a case using the "**Find**" command and send it to your printer, after which you want to sign off Westlaw. You would type the following:

fi	For find
22sct193	For the case citation indicated
pr	For printing
d	For all pages
atp	For attached printer
off	To sign off

Thus, by typing the following command,

fi22sct193; pr; d; atp; off

you can have Westlaw find the case indicated and send all pages of the case to your attached printer; then you will be signed off Westlaw. You may then go to the printer command and print the document after you have been signed off Westlaw, saving you the charges for the time it takes to print and find the document.

REVIEW QUESTIONS

1. What print options are available to you in Westlaw?
2. What destination options are available for printing?
3. What word processing options are available for printing?
4. What defaults are you able to set up for printing?
5. What is the command for printing offline? What is the advantage of doing so?
6. What command would you use to print a list of citations?
7. Define command stacking.

CHAPTER 5

Searching Databases— Case Law

A number of different databases are available within the Westlaw system. You will likely use the case law and statutes databases most often. However, additional databases are available for law review articles, journals, treatises, newspapers, news wires, and other news and information.

CASE LAW DATABASES

In addition to providing you with the actual case, the Westlaw system gives you editorial enhancements on that case. The *Full-Text Plus* format includes the following information in addition to the actual court opinion (see Figure 5-1, page 42):

1. *Synopsis field (sy)*—includes a summary of the case, consisting of a review of the facts of the case as well as the lower court judge's name and decision, the court's holding in the case itself, the name of the judge who wrote the court's opinion, any other judges who wrote or joined in dissenting or concurring opinions, and a syllabus of the case that has been prepared by the court, if available.

2. *Digest field (di)*—includes the headnotes and topics covered in the case.

3. *Topic field (to)*—includes the West key numbers that enable you to find cases with headnotes classified under a West digest topic. These topics have been separated into legal issues for identification purposes by West. Each issue is assigned a topic and key number classification.

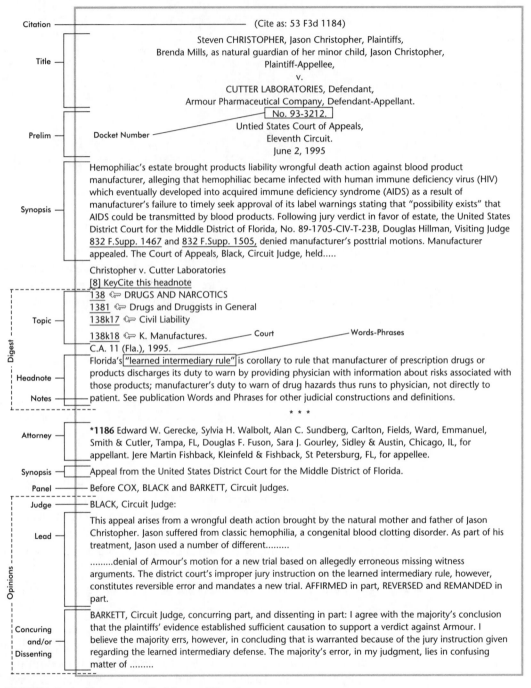

FIGURE 5-1 Case Law Fields on Westlaw

4. *Headnote field (he)*—includes headnotes for each point of law being decided in a case. Summaries are provided for each point of law in the case itself.

Methods of searching each of these parts of the database are discussed next. You may restrict your search to only one field or to a combination of fields.

SYNOPSIS FIELD SEARCH

There may be situations where you wish to obtain a review of the facts of several cases in order to choose those that are applicable to your own case. Or you may wish to find cases where a certain judge was reversed when the case was appealed to a higher court. You may wish to read opinions of certain judges to determine their rulings in certain types of cases. All of these tasks can be accomplished by searching the synopsis field in the following manner:

1. Go to the Terms & Connectors search page.
2. Click "Field Restrictions."
3. Select "Synopsis Sy" from the drop-down list.
4. Type your search terms.
5. Click "Go."

Alternatively, you may type

sy (term)

after your initial query in the Terms & Connectors query text box. Figure 5-2 on page 44 shows a typical synopsis field search result page.

DIGEST FIELD SEARCH

Use a digest field search when your terms have common words or multiple meanings, or when you want to restrict the result to a concept. The digest field search enables you to limit your search to the law in the digest. You are then able to find cases even if your request uses different terms from those used by the court in its decision.

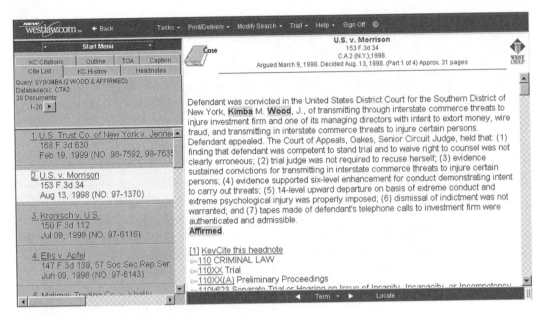

FIGURE 5-2 Synopsis Field Search Page

In order to search by the digest field alone, perform the following steps:

1. Go to the Terms & Connectors search page.
2. Click "Field Restrictions."
3. Select "Digest DI" from the drop-down list.
4. Type your search terms.
5. Click "Go."

If you wish to restrict your search terms to the same paragraph, use the connector for paragraph between your search terms **(/p)**.

Alternatively, just as in the synopsis field search, you may type

di

after your search terms in the query box to access the digest field.

In some cases, you may wish to search the synopsis and digest fields simultaneously. This technique is useful for finding only those cases where your terms are important. You can accomplish this task by typing

sy, di

before your search terms. Figure 5-3 shows a typical search page for a digest field search.

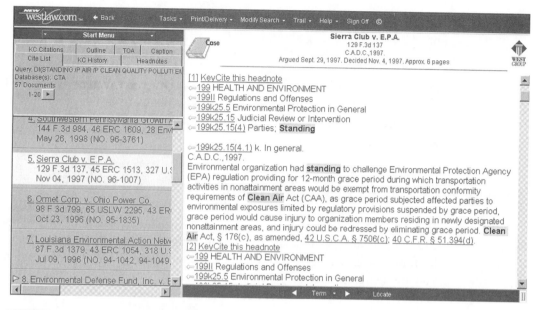

FIGURE 5-3 Digest Field Search Page

TOPIC SEARCHES

West assigns topics and key numbers to all cases in its national reporter system. By the use of these topics and key numbers, you can use West's publications and Westlaw together to find material. Restrict your search to West Digest topics or key numbers by following these directions:

1. Go to the Terms & Connectors search page.
2. Click "Field Restrictions."
3. Find the dialog box and select "Topic TO" from the drop-down list.
4. Scroll to the topic field access area and type your search terms in the box.
5. Click "Go."

Alternatively, you may type

to (terms)

after your initial search terms in the Terms & Connectors box. If you wish to use a key number instead of a digest topic, use the number after the "**to**." For example, you might use either

to(134)

or

to(divorce)

to find cases with headnotes for Topic 134, Divorce. If you wish to find
cases on two different topics, type both key numbers in the parentheses.
This search method is good for finding cases that discuss a certain specialty
area of the law.

SEARCHES BY HYPERTEXT LINK

Hypertext links are provided within the case headnotes to enable you to retrieve all headnotes in the appropriate jurisdiction that include that particular topic and key number. If you click the topic and key number in which
you are interested, you will be taken to the Key Number Center page (Figure 5-4). Use "Search" to find additional key numbers.

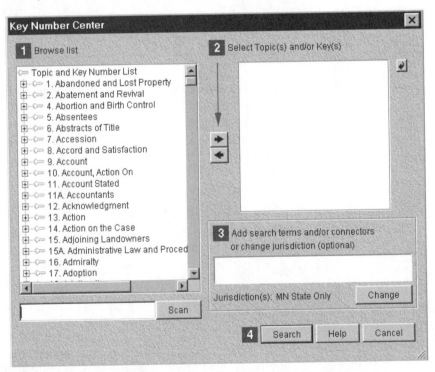

FIGURE 5-4 Key Search Page

Note that the jurisdiction displayed will always be your home jurisdiction. In the preceding example, the home jurisdiction is the state of Minnesota. If you wish to find material from other jurisdictions, you must so indicate by choosing an entry from the drop-down list.

You can also add additional terms to your search at this point. Type these terms in the box for "Additional Terms." The search will find those cases in the particular jurisdiction indicated.

CHANGING KEY NUMBERS

From time to time old key numbers are changed, deleted, or modified. New key numbers are added to accommodate the changes in the law. Your search will automatically take these changes into account so that if you enter an obsolete key number, Westlaw will update it to the revised number. In those cases, your search will indicate a new key number directly above the old one, with the word "Formerly" appearing next to the old key number. Figure 5-5 shows a key number search. Note that "Formerly" appears in the middle of the page under "Conspiracies."

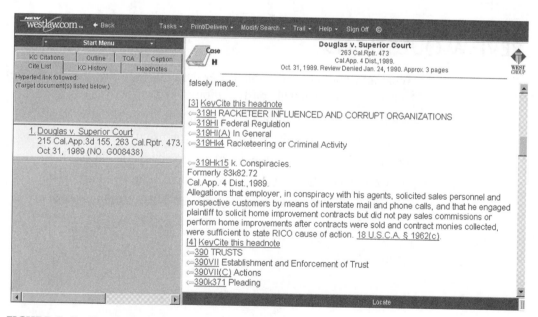

FIGURE 5-5 Headnote with "Formerly" Line

TABLE OF AUTHORITIES SERVICE

The Table of Authorities service enables you to find all other cases that have been cited by your case. It is a useful tool for determining if there are hidden weaknesses in the case you are using, because it lists all the cases on which the case you are using relied. It also shows any significant negative history of those cases. You can access the Table of Authorities service by the following steps:

1. Note the drop-down list at the top of the page.
2. Select "Table of Authorities," and click "Go."
3. The Table of Authorities page will be displayed. Type the case citation in the "Enter a Citation" box, and click "Go."

Cases will be listed by their citations and depth of history. (See Chapter 8 for an explanation of the star and flag codes used.) Cases with a negative history will be marked with red or yellow flags; those with a positive history will be marked with green flags.

Each number in the front of the citation represents a hyperlink to that case. Click the number of the case to view it.

REVIEW QUESTIONS

1. What information is available under the Full-Text Plus format of cases in addition to the actual court opinions?
2. What is a synopsis field search? When would you use it?
3. What is a digest search? When would you use it?
4. What would you type in the query box to access the digest field?
5. How do you conduct a topic search? When would you use it?
6. What is the Table of Authorities service? When would you use it?

CHAPTER

Searching Databases— Statutes

Westlaw enables you to search for both state and federal statutes and, in addition, find historical notes and annotations to assist you in an explanation and application of the statute. You may use "Scope" for basic information for research into statutes as well as descriptions of the database. This field is accessible by clicking the Scope icon: **i.**

USING FIND

If you know the exact number of the statute for which you are searching, use the following method to access the statute:

1. Find the drop-down list at the top of the page.
2. Click "Find a document" from the list.
3. Click "Go."
4. Type in the appropriate code for the statute being sought.

Specific instructions for retrieving federal and state statutes follow:

1. Retrieving federal statutes
   a. Go to the "Enter a citation" text box.
   b. Enter the citation.
   c. Click "Go."

For example, to retrieve 22 U.S.C.A. Sec. 994, type

22 usca s 994

and click "Go."

2. Retrieving state statutes
   a. Go to the "Enter a citation" text box.
   b. Type the state's postal abbreviation, statute abbreviation, and section.
   c. Click "Go."

For example, to retrieve a state statute for Florida with the number 222.11, type

fl st s 222.11

and click "Go."

3. Retrieving a state code (statute)
   a. Go to the "Enter a citation" text box.
   b. Type the state's postal abbreviation, code name or abbreviation, and code section number.
   c. Click "Go."

For example, to retrieve Section 211 of the Penal Code of California, type

ca p s 211

4. Retrieving a state constitution
   a. Go to the "Enter a citation" text box.
   b. Type the state abbreviation, constitution abbreviation, article and section numbers.
   c. Click "Go."

For example, to find Article 3, Section 9, of the Florida State Constitution, type

fl const art 3 s 9

A few states include both title and section numbers in their statutes. To retrieve one of their statutes, Step 4b under "Retrieving a state constitution" must include both the title and section number of the statute. For example, to find Title 22, Section 333, of Oklahoma State Statutes, type

ok st ti 22 s 333

or

ok st 22s333

SEARCHING WITHOUT CITATION

When you do not know the citation for a statute, you can do a descriptive word search by either the Terms & Connectors or Natural Language method.

Searching in an annotated statutes database will enable you to find how the statute has been construed and to obtain other information, including cases related to that particular statute. This method is particularly useful when you are searching for a term that is not usually found in statutory language.

SEARCHING WITH TABLE OF CONTENTS SERVICE

Suppose you are interested in viewing not only a particular statute but those statutes surrounding it as well. The Table of Contents service will provide those other statutes for you. This service is available for the following statutes:

1. United States Code Annotated (USCA)
2. Uniform Laws Annotated (ULA)
3. State statutes and rules (XX-ST)*
4. State administrative codes (XX-ADQ)*

Follow the following directions for finding statutes using this service:

1. Go to the drop-down list, and select "Table of Contents Service."
2. Click "Go."
3. Type the appropriate abbreviation for the material you wish to view.
4. Click "Go."

For example, if you wish to view the United States Code Annotated, type

usca

in Step 3, where you are supposed to type an abbreviation. If you wish to see all items available in the Table of Contents service, click "Abbreviations List" on the right side of the page (Figure 6-1, page 52).

---

* XX indicates the abbreviation for the particular state.

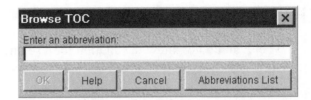

FIGURE 6-1 Table of Contents Service

You can also gain access to the Table of Contents service from a statute you are reading on your screen. If you click a heading in the statute's caption field, it will take you to the service (see Figures 6-2 and 6-3).

TOC Information Tab ————

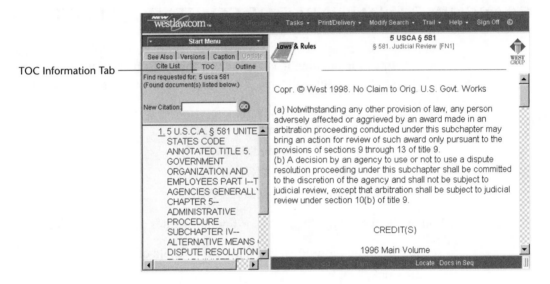

FIGURE 6-2 Statute Headings

Items available on the Table of Contents Service include the following:

1. Code of Federal Regulations
2. United States Code Annotated
3. Uniform Laws Annotated
4. State statutes
5. Court rules
6. Administrative materials

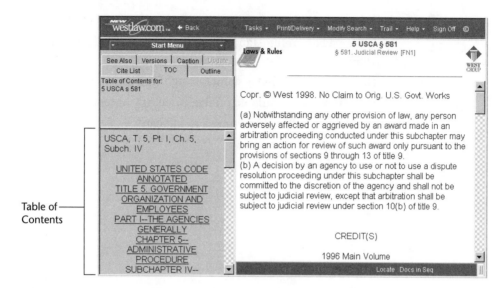

FIGURE 6-3   Title 5, USCA, Table of Contents

In some cases, the statute you retrieve will have been either amended or repealed. If so, you will see an "Update" message in the statute itself. To see the legislation that either amends or repeals your statute, click the "Update" hyperlink, and you will be taken to the new legislation.

New statutes can be retrieved via a legislative service database. These databases include laws that were passed during the present session of the legislature. They cannot be accessed via the Update link. Therefore, other methods must be used to update some of your research on statutes.

In those cases where a new statute has been enacted, it will be necessary to access a legislative service database and run a search using the appropriate issue being sought. To determine other uses of the legislative service database, or to find other databases dealing with statutes, use the Scope feature described earlier.

REVIEW QUESTIONS

1. Why would you use the Scope feature?
2. How do you find a statute if you have its citation?
3. How would you retrieve Florida statute No. 222.11?

4. How do you find a statute if you do not know its citation?

5. Under what circumstances would you use the Table of Contents service?

6. How would you find a statute using the Table of Contents service?

7. What items are available on the Table of Contents service?

8. What does an "Update" message indicate?

CHAPTER 7

Searching Databases— Secondary Sources

I n some cases, more general information is required in your research. Secondary sources (those representing persuasive authority or a comment about the law) may be accessed for explanations of legal principles in various fields. These sources are very useful for those situations where the researcher is unfamiliar with that area of the law and wishes to learn about that specialty and to find references to primary sources dealing with that practice area. Westlaw provides access to several hundred law reviews, state bar journals, course materials for continuing legal education, and newspapers for this type of research.

Several different types of databases are available to aid in your search of secondary sources. *General databases* provide a broad search capability in various secondary sources, such as textbooks, periodicals, law reviews, journals, newspapers, and other general information sources. *Specialty databases* provide information by law-specialty subject area, such as bankruptcy, estate planning, and family law. In addition, each journal and law review has its own database dating back to 1980. Figure 7-1 on page 56 shows a page of the Westlaw database directory for law reviews, practice guides, legal texts and periodicals.

Following are the identifiers for some of the general databases:

Database	Identifier
Law reviews, textbooks, and bar journals	TP-ALL
State journals and law reviews	XX-JLR*

---

* XX = state's abbreviation; e.g., CA-JLR would search for California's state bar journals.

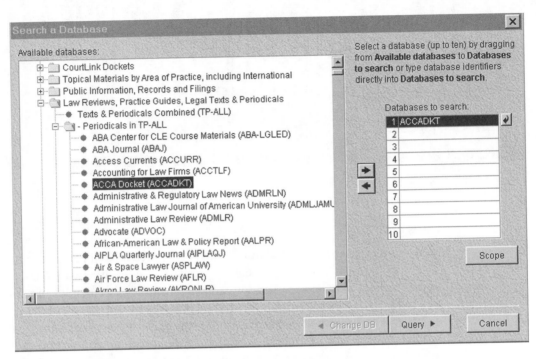

FIGURE 7-1 Law Reviews and Bar Journals Directory

Database	Identifier
American Bar Association journals	AMBAR-TP
American Law Institute of the ABA— continuing legal education	ALI-ABA
Textbooks and treatises on the law	TEXTS
United States newspapers	PAPERS PAPERS2
National Law Journal	NLJ

A list of databases available in various practice areas is presented in Figure 7-2. A list of databases for texts and treatises on the law, including all of the Restatement of the law, is given in Figure 7-3 on page 58. Note that these lists do not include all available databases. The online Westlaw Directory or the printed *Westlaw Database Directory* will give a complete list of all available secondary-source databases.

Database Name	Identifier
Administrative Law	AD-TP
Antitrust & Trade Regulation	ATR-TP
Bankruptcy	BKR-TP
Business Organizations	BUS-TP
Civil Rights	CIV-TP
Commercial Law & Contracts	CML-TP
Communications	COM-TP
Criminal Justice	CJ-TP
Education	ED-TP
Energy	EN-TP
Environmental Law	ENV-TP
Estate Planning & Probate	EPP-TP
Family Law	FL-TP
Finance & Banking	FIN-TP
First Amendment	CFA-TP
Government Benefits	GB-TP
Government Contracts	GC-TP
Health Law	HTH-TP
Immigration Law	IM-TP
Insurance	IN-TP
Intellectual Property	IP-TP
International Law	INT-TP
Jurisprudence & Constitutional Theory	JCT-TP
Labor & Employment	LB-TP
Legal Ethics & Professional Responsibility	ETH-TP
Litigation	LTG-TP
Maritime Law	MRT-TP
Military Law	MIL-TP

FIGURE 7-2 Specialty Topics Databases

Database Name	Identifier
Native Americans Law	NAM-TP
Pension & Retirement Benefits	PEN-TP
Products Liability	PL-TP
Professional Malpractice	MAL-TP
Real Property	RP-TP
Securities and Blue Sky Law	SEC-TP
Taxation	TX-TP
Tort Law	TRT-TP
Transportation	TRAN-TP
Workers' Compensation	WC-TP

FIGURE 7-2 (*continued*)

Database Name	Identifier
American Law Reports	ALR
Clean Air Act: Law and Practice	JW-CLEANAIR
Couch on Insurance	COUCH
Environmental Law	ENVLAW
Federal Jury Practice and Instructions	FED-JI
Federal Practice and Procedure	FPP
Federal Sentencing Law and Practice	FSLP
Federal Tax Practice (Casey)	CASEY
Handbook of Federal Evidence	FEDEVID
Handbook on Insurance Coverage Disputes	ICD
Hazardous Waste Law and Practice	JW-HAZWASTE
Law of Federal Income Taxation (Mertens)	MERTENS
Manual for Complex Litigation	MCL
Modern Intellectual Property, Second Edition	MODIP

FIGURE 7-3   Restatement, Text, and Treatise Databases

Database Name	Identifier
Principles of Corporate Governance: Analysis and Recommendations	ALI-CORPGOV
Punitive Damages: A State-by-State Guide to Law and Practice	PUNITIVE
Restatements of the Law	REST
Agency	REST-AGEN
Conflict of Laws	REST-CONFL
Contracts	REST-CONTR
Foreign Relations Law of the United States, The	REST-FOREL
Judgments	REST-JUDG
Law Governing Lawyers, The	REST-LGOVL
Property	REST-PROP
Restitution	REST-RESTI
Security and Suretyship and Guaranty	REST-SEC
Torts	REST-TORT
Trusts	REST-TRUST
Unfair Competition	REST-UNCOM
Search and Seizure: A Treatise on the Fourth Amendment	SEARCHSZR
Treatise on Constitutional Law: Substance and Procedure	CONLAW
Uniform Commercial Code Series (Hawkland)	HAWKLAND
Witkin's California Treatises	WITKIN

FIGURE 7-3   (*continued*)

INDEX TO LEGAL PERIODICALS/ LEGAL RESOURCE INDEX

The Index to Legal Periodicals (ILP) and the Legal Resource Index (LRI) contain lists of articles on given subjects from all over the world. You can use a Natural Language search method with them to search for all articles on a particular subject. For instance, if you wish to find articles on surrogate parenting in the LRI database, you would perform the following steps:

1. Access the LRI database.

2. Note that you wish to use the Natural Language search method.

3. Enter the following explanation in the terms field:

surrogate parenting

You will be able to retrieve up to 100 articles on surrogate parenting that have appeared in journals in the United States, Great Britain, Australia, Canada, New Zealand, and Ireland. A Terms & Connectors search for

surrogate /5 parent! mother!

will generate over 900 documents. See Figure 7-4 for a sample search result using the LRI.

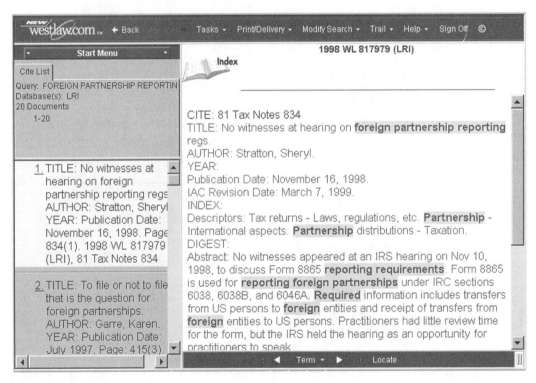

FIGURE 7-4 Legal Resource Index (LRI) Search Result

FINDING LAW REVIEW ARTICLES

Just as statutes and cases can be retrieved using "Find" (discussed earlier), law review articles can also be found in this manner provided you know the citation for the article. Perform the following steps:

1. From the top of the page, select "Find a document" from the drop-down list.
2. Click "Go."
3. Note the "Enter a citation" box, type the citation for the law review article you are seeking.

If that particular law review is not available, another page will appear indicating whether the article summary can be accessed in the (LRI) database or the Index to Legal Periodicals (ILP).

In order to determine whether the particular publication in which you are interested is accessible, you can also use the "Find" feature:

1. Select "Find."
2. Click "Publications List" on the left side of the screen.
3. A list of all publications available on Westlaw will be shown.

To find a list of only law reviews accessible, click the "Contains" button on the top of the page after performing the preceding three steps. When the text box appears, type

law reviews

and click "Scan." A sample page using this feature is shown in Figure 7-5 on page 62.

Several other search methods are available for publications. You can search for articles by the author's name, the title of the article, or by subject. These methods were discussed earlier for statutes and cases. They are the same for articles or publications.

To utilize these procedures for searching, you must first access the appropriate publication or law review database. Once the database has been found, use these steps to find the article in which you are interested.

1. Author's Name
   a. Access the appropriate database.
   b. Select the Terms & Connectors search method.

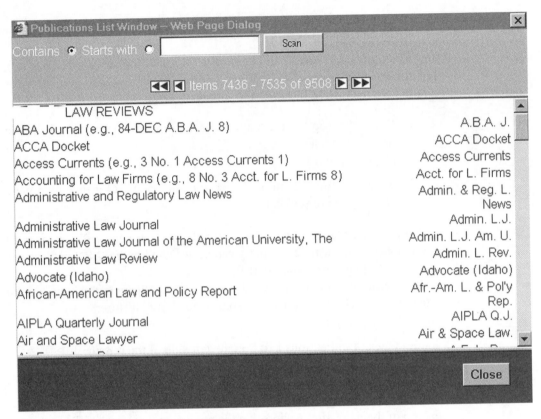

FIGURE 7-5 Law Reviews Search Using Scan

      c. Restrict your search to the author field (au).

      d. Enter your query for the author.

  2. Title of article

      a. Access the appropriate database.

      b. Select the Terms & Connectors search method.

      c. Restrict your search to the title field (ti).

      d. Enter your query for the name of the article.

  3. Subject of article

      a. Access the appropriate database.

      b. Select the Natural Language search method.

      c. Type in a description of the subject in which you are interested.

You may need to review the search procedures for Natural Language and Terms & Connectors from Chapter 5.

Often when you are reading a case or law review article, you will find a hypertext link to another article. You can instantly access that article by clicking on the hypertext link.

HIGHLIGHTS DATABASES

On occasion you will wish to view the recent legal developments in a given area of law, in a certain state, or from the United States Supreme Court. The following databases enable you to conduct this type of search:

1. *Westlaw Bulletin (WLB)*—This database provides a brief description of recent cases on the state and federal levels.

2. *Topical Highlights*—Descriptions are provided for recent cases in given legal specialty areas, such as probate, family law, or bankruptcy.

3. *State Bulletins*—Significant cases decided by specific states are described.

4. *Westlaw Bulletin for the United States Supreme Court (WLB-SCT)*— Recent Supreme Court issues and developments are provided, as well as cases, orders, and court rules.

For additional lists of Topical Highlights databases, see the Westlaw Directory.

NEWS AND GENERAL INFORMATION DATABASES

Sometimes you must search more general information sources to find background information and foundational data. Many general sources are available on Westlaw—newspapers, news wires, newsletters, journals, and magazines. Over 1,000 newspapers may be accessed via Westlaw. A complete directory of all such databases can be found on the online Westlaw Directory or the *Westlaw Data Directory.* To obtain a detailed description of the database, see "Scope."

Newspaper databases can provide information relevant to your issue by means of news stories related to lawsuits that have been settled. You can find information about a particular attorney, a particular lawsuit, a certain trial, or lawsuits involving a specific company.

NEWS WIRES

The Dow Jones news wire databases are particularly valuable to attorneys dealing in international law, corporate law, government law, or finance. News about companies in the United States, Japan, Germany, Asia, and Canada can be obtained, including financial information and stock market data on those countries. Government law offices will find information about government agencies to be useful.

Detailed information about corporations is available regarding the following:

1. Mergers and acquisitions
2. Tender offers
3. Proxies
4. Prospectuses
5. Leveraged buyouts
6. Current filings with the Securities and Exchange Commission (SEC)

Many Dow Jones databases are found in the Dow Jones Wires database (WIRES).

If you want to find news stories that were added to a particular database within the last few hours, type **"read"** or **"list"** in the Terms & Connectors query text box, and only those articles will appear. When retrieving articles about a given subject, you can restrict your search to a certain time period, or a particular area in the databases, such as the type of industry, ticker symbol, or company name. You may also use "Locate" to get the articles you want in WIRES.

One of the health law databases, such as MEDLINE, is particularly useful to attorneys, paralegals, legal nurse consultants, and others who are employed in the area of medical malpractice. MEDLINE contains articles describing various medical procedures as well as the related law.

Attorneys practicing corporate law may be interested in information on mergers or acquisitions. The *Wall Street Journal* (WSJ) database contains this information. In order to find information about the merger of Lucky and Albertson stores, for example, perform the following steps:

1. Access the *Wall Street Journal* database (WSJ).
2. Type the following information in the query box:

    lucky /p albertson

3. The result will be all articles containing those names within the same paragraph.

Corporate financial information is valuable for firms that have business dealings with these corporations. This material is available in the "Disclosure" database. Suppose you wish to find financial information about General Motors Corporation. Use the following query:

1. Access the SECNOW database for SEC filings.
2. Type the name of the company in which you are interested in the box.

SEC filings or financial information for that company will be found.

THE WESTCLIP SERVICE FOR CURRENT EVENTS

The WestClip service enables you to keep up to date on current events and legal developments that affect your practice area of law. You may run a Terms & Connectors query and receive information from this clipping service on a regular basis. The results of the search are delivered to you automatically. In order to activate this service, perform the following steps:

1. Select "WestClip Directory" from the drop-down list at the top of the page, and click "Go." The right frame will show an overview of WestClip.
2. Click "Entry Wizard" in the left frame on your screen. The wizard will help you create a new entry.

If you have already formulated a Terms & Connectors query, perform the following steps:

1. Select "Add to WestClip" from the drop-down list and click "Go." The query will be added to the Entry Wizard.

2. Follow the instructions in the wizard to select a frequency setting, next run date, delivery format and destination, and name for the entry.

3. Click "Finish."

REVIEW QUESTIONS

1. What secondary sources are found in general databases?

2. What are specialty databases?

3. What is the identifier for bar journals?

4. Where can you find a complete list of all available secondary source databases?

5. How would you find a law review article if you have its citation?

6. Where can you find recent Supreme Court developments? What is the identifier of this database?

7. What information can you find about corporations in the Dow Jones News wire databases?

8. Where would you find information about corporate mergers?

CHAPTER 8

KeyCite

 ecall the many hours spent updating cases using books, and you will appreciate the new Westlaw feature called KeyCite, which is one of the most current, comprehensive, accurate and easy-to-use citation updating systems. KeyCite allows you to automatically monitor changes in cases and statutes in which you are interested merely by clicking your mouse. It integrates all case law on Westlaw and enables you to trace the history of a case, retrieve a list of all cases citing that case, track legal issues in a case, and find case discussions by legal experts.

KeyCite covers all federal and state cases in West's reporter systems, along with more than 1 million unpublished cases and over 600 law reviews. Federal case history begins with the earliest reported cases in 1754. State case history begins with 1879. It also includes thousands of *American Jurisprudence 2d* articles, *Couch on Insurance,* Merten's *Law of Federal Taxation, Norton on Bankruptcy Law and Practice 2d,* Rutter Group publications, Witkin's *California Law* materials, and Wright and Miller's *Federal Practice and Procedure.*

EVALUATING CASE LAW

A considerable amount of time and effort needs to be spent in the evaluation of case law in order to determine the following:

1. Is this case "good law"?
2. What is the history of this case?
3. Which other cases have cited this case?
4. What are the relevant legal issues in this case?

5. Which other cases deal with these issues?

6. What other relevant material supports the cited cases?

7. Which other cases are cited by this case?

8. Are all the cited cases that have cited this case "good law"?

UPDATING CASES WITH BOOKS

Citator books may have several volumes and monthly supplements that are very expensive. Maintenance is cumbersome and tedious. In order to update a case or statute, several volumes of the books must be reviewed, a process that can take several hours of your time. Yet, information is only as current as your last updated volume, which may be up to a month old.

Cases and statutes are listed by citation only without the case names. The following process is used:

1. Review the citation for the case or statute you are updating.

2. Find the appropriate volume of the citator for your case or statute.

3. Look up the citation and review all subsequent citations listed.

4. If you are updating to find whether the case is "good law" (that is, whether it has been overruled), look for that code "O" below the main case.

5. Find the case or statute that overrules yours.

6. Check all subsequent volumes of the citator series; perform Steps 1 through 5 for each supplement.

7. Note the date of the latest supplement. Any cases decided after that date will not appear.

UPDATING WITH KEYCITE

Access to KeyCite can be obtained by any one of the following methods:

1. Use the Westlaw pull-down menu.

2. Click the graphic KC icon in your Westlaw toolbar.

3. Click on a status flag, described shortly, from a case display on Westlaw.

4. Click on "KeyCite this headnote" if you are in a headnote in Westlaw.

See Figure 8-1 for Accessing KeyCite.

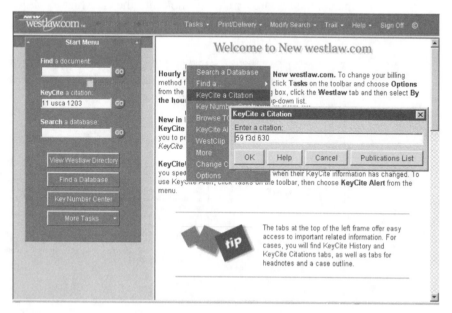

FIGURE 8-1   Accessing KeyCite

Some law firms require that all citations be rechecked on another system or by using the books (*Shepard's*).

SPECIAL FEATURES OF KEYCITE

A number of unique features are found within the KeyCite system. Case histories are available within KeyCite the same day they appear in Westlaw. Each citing case links the headnotes of all cases referenced within them using topics and key numbers. A unique graphical display enables you to find information quickly.

A system using red and yellow flags enables you to quickly determine any negative history about the case. The red flag means that the case is no longer "good law" because it has been overruled, reversed, vacated, or abrogated. The yellow flag means the case has some negative history but it has not been overruled or reversed. The presence of a blue "H" means that the case has some history. All of these flags are linked to the appropriate case citations as soon as the case appears on Westlaw. Any time a flag appears, the researcher should look into the case history. Figure 8-2 shows the different categories of history.

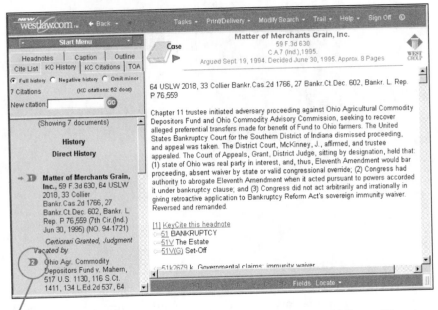

Click the retrieval number of an item listed in the left frame to view the full text of the document in the Link Viewer.

FIGURE 8-2 Case Categories

The red flag accompaniment to a statute means it has been either amended or repealed. A yellow flag means there is pending legislation that may affect the statute.

Green stars show which cases discuss the instant case the most so the reader can focus on what later courts have said. Starting with those cases with the most stars enables you to learn the most about a case in the least amount of time. Figure 8-3 on page 71 shows the definitions of the different numbers of green stars.

One may think of the stars as being analogous to the positive history of the case and the flags to the negative history.

Depth of Treatment Categories		
Examined	★★★★	The citing case contains an extended discussion of the cited case, usually more than a printed page of text.
Discussed	★★★	The citing case contains a substantial discussion of the cited case, usually more than a paragraph but less than a printed page.
Cited	★★	The citing case contains some discussion of the cited case, usually less than a paragraph.
Mentioned	★	The citing case contains a brief reference to the cited case, usually in a string citation.

FIGURE 8-3 Definitions of Green Stars in KeyCite

CUSTOMIZING YOUR KEYCITE DISPLAY

The KeyCite system has a method for restricting your research. You may select the full history of the case, only the negative history, or omit the minor history.

Suppose you are about to file an appellate brief with the court. The brief contains many case citations and it must be submitted to the court today. You would likely wish to check only negative history for each case cited in your brief.

Note that all case names are shown in their entirety. Both the name of the case and its citation are displayed.

KEY NUMBERING SYSTEM

The West key numbering system has been fully integrated into the KeyCite system, hence the word "Key" in its name. Citations can be displayed by both topic and West key number for your own jurisdiction. After you find the proper key number for your case or issue, you can be assured that all relevant cases will be displayed.

VIEWING A KEYCITE CASE HISTORY

Once you find the case in which you are interested in the KeyCite system, the history of the case will be displayed. It is divided into the following sections:

1. *Direct history*—This section traces the history of the case through the appellate process and includes prior and subsequent history.

2. *Negative indirect history*—This section lists cases outside the direct appellate line that might have a negative impact on the instant case.

3. *Related references*—This section lists cases involving the same parties and facts as your case, including those with different legal issues.

VIEWING CASE CITATIONS

Once you have access to the KeyCite display for your particular case, you can view all cases and secondary sources that cite your case. Click "Citations to the Case" in the left frame of the History of the Case display. A list of citations will be given.

Negative cases that cited your case are listed first. Then all other cases citing your case follow, categorized by the depth of treatment they give your case. The star system just discussed indicates the depth of treatment.

LIMITING YOUR RESEARCH

Figure 8-4 on page 73 shows the screen that appears if you click "Other Limits" in KeyCite. Several different limitations are possible to further restrict the information you are seeking.

Following are the restrictions available as noted in Figure 8-4:

1. You can restrict your search to either headnotes or topics by clicking the appropriate box. In this particular case, the researcher is interested in the topic "Attorney and Client."

2. A particular jurisdiction or West publication provides a further limitation. In this case, the researcher is interested in California materials only.

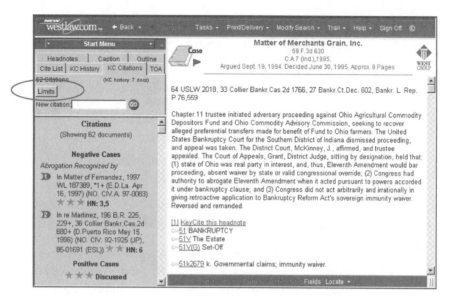

FIGURE 8-4   KeyCite's Other Limitations

3. The type of document in which you are interested should be checked under this section. This researcher is interested in opinions of the highest courts as well as many secondary sources.

4. By the use of the document dates field, the search can be restricted by a specific time period.

5. Note the green-star system discussed earlier. Checking the green-star boxes limits the search to the most relevant cases.

6. If you wish to know how often this case was cited as well as the average number of citations for the same year and jurisdiction, check this box. In this case, 67 out of 242 documents cited the subject case.

KEYCITE ALERT

A recent addition to the KeyCite system is a tracking device for keeping you informed of important developments that affect relevant cases and statutes. The KeyCite Alert informs you automatically of any changes or updates in the particular area of interest. Limits can be made based on

1. Negative history (the red and yellow flag system)

2. Treatment depth (the green star system)

3. Headnotes or legal issues
4. Specific jurisdictions
5. Notes of decisions
6. Time limits

See Figure 8-5 on page 75 for a KeyCite Alert system entry using the following descriptions:

1. Frequency option and place of delivery
2. Searching limitations
3. Headnotes and topics limits
4. Depth of treatment (green stars)

In the given example, the researcher is interested in a daily notification by e-mail of the full text of documents under Headnote "(5)States" for keynote number 4.1(1) for Minnesota from the highest courts, as well as secondary sources with the depth entry for three and four green stars.

REVIEW QUESTIONS

1. What is KeyCite?
2. What does KeyCite cover?
3. How do you gain access to KeyCite?
4. What do yellow and red flags signify?
5. Once you have access to the KeyCite display for your particular case, how can you find all cases and secondary sources that cite your case?
6. What is the tracking device for keeping you informed of important developments that affect relevant cases and statutes?

Using KeyCite Alert to Monitor Citations

KeyCite Alert automatically monitors the status of cases and statutes and sends you updates when their KeyCite information changes. When you create a KeyCite Alert entry, you specify how frequently your case or statute should be checked: daily, every weekday, weekly, biweekly or monthly. KeyCite Alert can deliver results to an attached or stand-alone printer, fax machine or e-mail address or download the results to disk. You can also choose to save your result on Westlaw for 30 days and access the results in the Offline Print Directory.

To access KeyCite Alert and create an entry, click **Tasks** on the toolbar and choose **KeyCite Alert**, **Create Entry (Standard)** or **Create Entry (Wizard)**. To view your KeyCite Alert Directory, choose **KeyCite Alert**, **View KeyCite Alert Directory**.

When you choose **KeyCite Alert**, **Create Entry (Wizard)**, a dialog box provides step-by-step guidance in creating a KeyCite Alert entry.

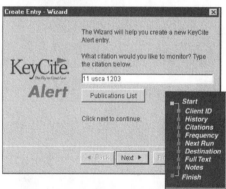

The KeyCite Alert Directory lists the entries you have created in the order in which you saved them. You can use the Directory to view, edit or delete entries. Highlight an entry in the KeyCite Alert Directory, then click **View/Edit** or **Delete**.

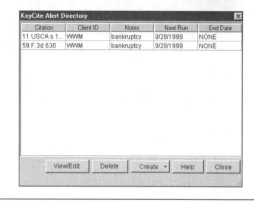

FIGURE 8-5 KeyCite Alert System

PART II
Westlaw Using Westmate

CHAPTER 9

Installing Westmate

Those individuals who prefer to work with a software package not connected to the Internet may use the Westmate system for Windows 95 and Windows NT. This package is provided by West and customizes your computer for Westlaw research. Some of the features of Westmate 7.1 include the following:

1. The system is designed for Windows 95 and Windows NT 4.0 or higher and is compatible with Microsoft Office 97.
2. It utilizes a Windows 95 graphical interface.
3. It provides right mouse button navigation as well as tabular dialog boxes and controls.
4. It maintains the ability to access West Group's Web sites.
5. It provides a context-sensitive Help system as well as automatic installation and removal.
6. It furnishes added accessibility for persons with disabilities.

The Westmate software is sent on a CD-ROM along with the *Westmate Technical Reference Manual* and a guide, *Using Westmate,* by West. More information is provided about Westlaw documents at the Web site:

http://www.westgroup.com/wlawinfo/wlawdoc

HELP FILE

An extensive Help system is provided to answer questions about Westmate and Westlaw without the necessity of signing on to Westlaw. A complete index and glossary of terms are provided. They provide the ability to access the West Group Web page on the Internet directly from the Help menu. Context-sensitive help is furnished in pop-up windows by when you use the right mouse button or press F1. Text can be copied from the Help file to your Clipboard by means of the copy-and-paste feature.

INSTALLATION EQUIPMENT REQUIREMENTS

In order to run Westmate on your computer, you must have the following features:

1. Windows 95 or Windows NT 4.0 or higher

2. VGA or Super VGA monitor

3. 486/25 or Pentium, with Pentium preferred

4. 12MB of memory if running Windows 95 (4MB minimum); 20MB of memory if running Windows NT (16MB minimum)

5. Mouse or other pointing device

6. CD-ROM drive

7. 14,400 bps modem or higher (9,600 bps minimum); or LAN communications server (TCP/IP, Eicon)

INSTALLATION PROCEDURE

The Westmate CD-ROM disk must be inserted into your CD-ROM drive to begin the installation. Click "Next" to start the installation program automatically. If it will not start, choose "Run" from your "Start" menu, and locate your CD-ROM drive, then choose "Setup."

When the Westmate dialog box appears, choose "Next" to install the program to the Destination Folder indicated on your screen. If you wish to select a different destination, or if you are installing Westmate on a network, click "Browse" to select the appropriate destination. Then click "Next."

The Communication Setup dialog box will appear. Click "Next" if you wish to have Westmate automatically detect the appropriate communications device; otherwise check the box that says "Don't detect. ..."

Throughout the installation process, a series of pages will appear asking you whether you wish this particular item to be used and offering an alternative on the page itself. If all items are correct, continue to click "Next" until installation is complete. Then click "Finish."

REVIEW QUESTIONS

1. What system requirements do you need to install Westmate?
2. Explain how to install Westmate on your system.

CHAPTER 10

Starting Westlaw Using Westmate

Prior to beginning your research session, you must establish a connection to Westlaw as follows:

1. Click the "Start" button.

2. Choose "Programs," then "West Applications," and then "Westmate."

3. You will see the dialog box for signing on Westlaw. Type your password and client ID into the boxes provided for that purpose.

4. Select a dialing location from the drop-down list entitled "My Location" if you are using a local modem.

5. Check the appropriate billing method, either hourly or transactional.

6. Click "OK."

7. The "Welcome to New Westlaw" screen will appear.

SIGNING OFF WESTLAW

When you are ready to exit from the Westlaw system, sign off as follows:

1. Find the File menu and choose "Sign off Westlaw."

2. Click the proper button if you wish to save the current project on which you are working.

3. You will see the Westlaw Time Summary box that indicates how much time you have been online with Westlaw. You are not yet disconnected from the system at this point.

4. Click "OK."

5. To exit from Westmate, choose "Exit" from your File menu.

CUSTOMIZING WESTMATE

Westmate provides the capability to make changes in the system to customize its use for your own particular needs. You can change your documents display, the text type, fonts, and color of text, and your file storage.

To change how items appear on your screen, choose "Options" from the Tools menu. Star paging display options enable you to display pagination from printed publications obtained on Westlaw.

To change the text type, font, font size, and color of text in documents, choose "Fonts" from "Options" in the Tools menu. To change the location for storage of your files—that is to choose a different download folder—click "File Locations" from "Options". A dialog box will appear. You may also save specific queries and actions in a separate project folder.

PASSWORD STORAGE

When you sign on to Westlaw, you will see a box marked "Remember Password." If you check this box, you will not have to retype your password each time you sign on to Westlaw. However, if your password is stored, anyone using your computer will be able to sign on to Westlaw automatically with your stored password.

COMMUNICATIONS OPTIONS

With the use of the Westmate software, you can set up communications options for accessing Westlaw, specify sign-on options, and modify advanced communications access. Most people will, however, find the default settings that have already been provided with the system satisfactory.

If you are using a local modem, you should set up the general communications from "Communications Options" in the Tools (or Files) menu. The page will display a drop-down list of modems or other communications devices, such as Internet TCP/IP or Eicon. Select your modem from the list.

ACCESSING WESTMATE FROM ANOTHER LOCATION

In order to access Westlaw from another place, click "Dialing Properties" in the Communications Setup—General dialog box. Select the number and area code as well as any numbers that must be dialed to access an outside line. Clicking "Phone Numbers" from "Communications Options" will enable you to determine the current access phone numbers.

In order to add a telephone number, click "Next" and specify your current location. Click "Next" again, and you will be able to retrieve telephone numbers for your current location.

REVIEW QUESTIONS

1. How do you sign onto Westlaw using Westmate?
2. How do you sign off Westlaw using Westmate?
3. How can you customize your screen using Westmate?

CHAPTER 11

Using Westmate

After you have installed Westmate on your computer, you will notice an icon for Westmate on your desktop. Double-click on this icon to enter the Westlaw system.

You will notice a "Tip of the Day" box giving you a hint on how to use a particular function. Click "Close" to access the "Sign on to New Westlaw" screen. Type in your password and client identifier, and click "OK."

STARTING YOUR RESEARCH

The principles used with Westmate are the same as those used when you are accessing Westlaw via the Internet. Many of the Web pages look the same. The "Welcome to New Westlaw" window enables you to start the following tasks by choosing items:

1. Click your right mouse button; choose an item from the pop-up menu.

2. Select the drop-down menu; choose an item from it.

3. Click one of the buttons on the left side of the window to

   a. Search for a database.

   b. Display a customized list of databases.

   c. Verify with KeyCite.

   d. Find a document by citation.

   e. Display your saved queries in the WestClip directory.

   f. Search for a key number and topic using the key numbering system.

4. If you know the identifier for the database, type it in the "Database" window and click "Search."

Three methods are available to execute a command on Westmate:

1. Icon on the button bar
2. Pull-down menu bar
3. Buttons on the left on the Main Menu.

MAIN BUTTON TOOLBAR

Most Westmate windows display a button toolbar at the top of the screen. The buttons and their functions are given in Figure 11-1 on page 89. If the toolbar is displayed on the screen, you can click on one of the buttons to perform the described function.

BOOKMARKS AND FAVORITE PLACES

You may already be familiar with *bookmarks,* the feature which allows you to mark favorite Web sites to which you wish to return frequently. This feature is also available in the Westmate system so that you can store the databases or services that you use most often. Use one of the following methods to access it:

1. Click "Favorite Places" from the list that appears when you click your right mouse button.
2. Access the "Research" menu, and click "Favorite Places."
3. From the "Welcome to New Westlaw" screen, choose "Favorite Places" from the left side of the screen.
4. From the Main Menu page, choose "Favorite Places" from the buttons displayed.

Once the list for Favorite Places is displayed on your screen, you may add the database to your list, choose a list from the list of state or practice-area templates, or find databases to add to the list in the Westlaw Directory.

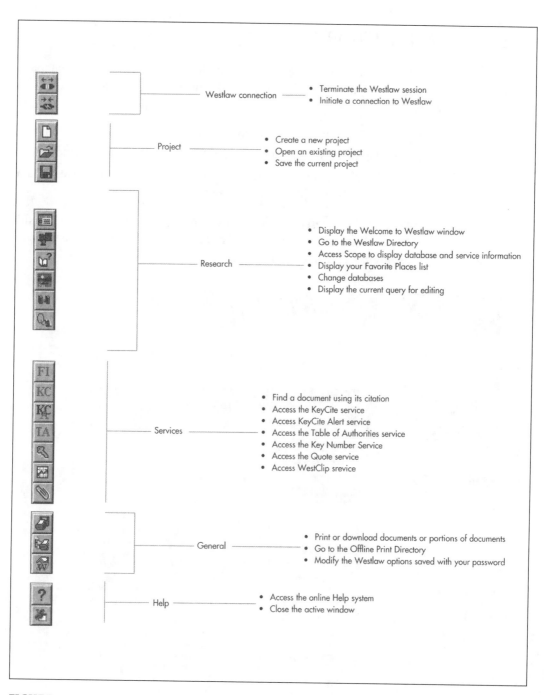

FIGURE 11-1   Main Button Toolbar in Westmate

WESTLAW DIRECTORY

The Westlaw Directory provides a list of all Westlaw services and databases in the form of an index. This directory can be accessed in three different ways:

1. In the "Search" or "Research" menu, choose "Westlaw Directory."
2. On the Main Screen, click on the "Westlaw Directory" button.
3. On the "Welcome to New Westlaw" page, click "Choose a Database" on the left side of the screen.

Once you have accessed the Westlaw Directory, the icons on the left side of the list enable you to view its subsections. Click an icon for a list of subsections. Figure 11-2 shows an example of the Westlaw directory.

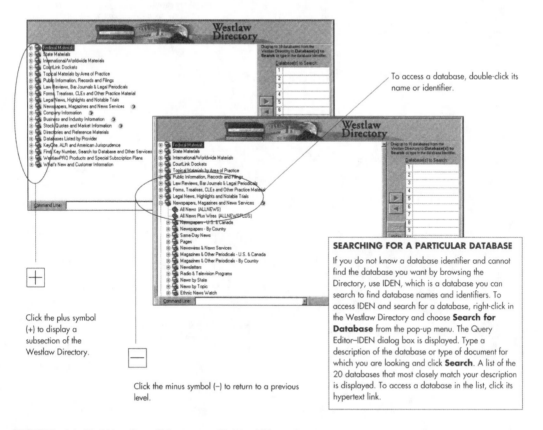

To access a database, double-click its name or identifier.

Click the plus symbol (+) to display a subsection of the Westlaw Directory.

Click the minus symbol (–) to return to a previous level.

SEARCHING FOR A PARTICULAR DATABASE

If you do not know a database identifier and cannot find the database you want by browsing the Directory, use IDEN, which is a database you can search to find database names and identifiers. To access IDEN and search for a database, right-click in the Westlaw Directory and choose **Search for Database** from the pop-up menu. The Query Editor–IDEN dialog box is displayed. Type a description of the database or type of document for which you are looking and click **Search**. A list of the 20 databases that most closely match your description is displayed. To access a database in the list, click its hypertext link.

FIGURE 11-2 Westlaw Directory Using Westmate

Note that the "Scope" option is available from Westmate. This option enables you to see the specific features of the particular database or service. It can be accessed in one of the following ways:

1. Click "Scope" from the pop-up menu that appears when you click your right mouse button.
2. Note the buttons on the main page and click "Scope."

To exit the Scope feature, click the button to close the window that is located in the upper-right corner of the window.

RETRIEVING DOCUMENTS BY CITATION

You can retrieve documents by using their citation with the "Find" feature. In order to access "Find," perform one of the following steps:

1. From the "Welcome to New Westlaw" page, click "Find a Document" on the left side of the screen.
2. From the Main Page, click "Find a Document" from the button bar.
3. Choose "Find a Document" from the list that appears when you click your right mouse button.
4. Click "Find a Document" from the "Services" (or "Research") menu.

Once you are on the "Find" page, the methods for finding documents are similar to those described earlier (page 16). Type your citation in the text box, and click "OK."

Documents that can be retrieved with the "Find" feature include federal and state statutes, federal and state case law, administrative decisions, law reviews, legal periodicals, and news items. Some examples of retrievable items and their citations follow:

United States Supreme Court cases	215 sct 1133
Federal Rules of Evidence	fre 333
Article from *Time Magazine*	3/6/99 timemag 11
Harvard Law Review Article	32 harv l rev 366

CONDUCTING SEARCHES

Chapter 3 provides a detailed description of how to find documents using a Natural Language or Terms & Connectors search. The same methods are used with Westmate.

SURVEYING RETRIEVED DOCUMENTS

Once you have conducted a search, the case or other document will appear on your screen. The right mouse button is used to perform the following navigation functions:

1. Move between pages of the document.
2. Go to a list of documents found.
3. Edit your original query.
4. Locate the point at which particular terms appear in the document.
5. Send the document to a printer or disk to be copied.
6. Update the document appearing on the screen if it is a statute.

Figure 11-3 on page 93 shows a Westmate page after a search has been conducted, with the pop-up menu that appears when you click the right mouse button appearing on the right side of the screen.

Note the toolbar or pull-down menu at the top of the screen display. The arrow keys can be used to move to the "Previous" or "Next" search term or document. Other functions are explained within the toolbar itself.

The title of the window at the top of the screen indicates the database that was searched as well as the description you used to find the document indicated. Note the large arrow in the middle of the screen or flags displayed at the top of the screen. This arrow indicates that negative or positive history will be available in the KeyCite system, as described earlier in Chapter 8.

Hypertext links are available at the bottom of the page for purposes of moving to other locations in Westlaw. If you click the "Page" or "Document" box on the bottom of the screen, you will be able to immediately go to the next page or document. Use the right mouse button or "Go to" command to navigate to a specific page or document.

The window title indicates the database searched and the description or query used to retrieve the result.

A red or yellow flag indicates that negative history for this case is available in KeyCite.

Click a hypertext link to move to another location on Westlaw.

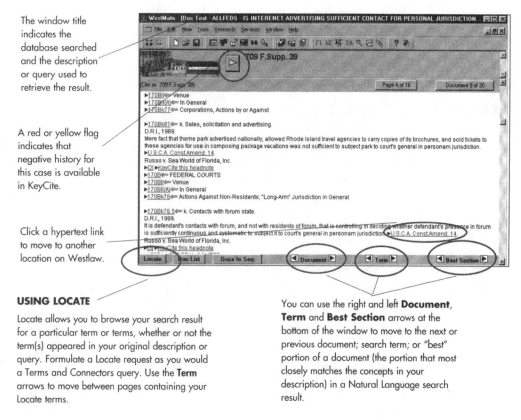

FIGURE 11-3   Document Window Display

USING LOCATE

Locate allows you to browse your search result for a particular term or terms, whether or not the term(s) appeared in your original description or query. Formulate a Locate request as you would a Terms and Connectors query. Use the **Term** arrows to move between pages containing your Locate terms.

You can use the right and left **Document**, **Term** and **Best Section** arrows at the bottom of the window to move to the next or previous document; search term; or "best" portion of a document (the portion that most closely matches the concepts in your description) in a Natural Language search result.

LISTING DOCUMENTS

The method used for viewing a list of citations obtained from your particular search is the same as that described in Chapter 3 under "Surveying Retrieved Documents."

Alternatively, if you click the right mouse button, you will see a list from which you can choose the following functions, depending on your version of Westlaw:

1. See the full document.
2. See a summary of your search result.
3. Locate items within the documents.

4. Print or download items.

5. Change the order in which documents are shown. (Note: You may need to use the Options menu.)

ORGANIZING PROJECTS

One major advantage of using Westmate is the ability to organize your research sessions into folders for future use. Each research session is stored in an electronic folder called a "project" that can be accessed at a later date. These projects can be separated by client identifier. Projects are stored in a "Project Log" that is accessed by choosing "Project" from the "View" menu.

SAVING PROJECTS

Before you sign off Westlaw, you should either (1) choose "Save Project" from the File menu or (2) click the button titled "Save Project" on the main button toolbar. Just as you save files on your computer, you would then type an identification into the File Name box. Up to eight characters can be used. Click "Save," and the project will be saved to the project file unless you specify another directory in which you would like your project placed.

CREATING NEW PROJECTS DURING RESEARCH SESSION

Each time you sign on to Westlaw using Westmate, new projects are created automatically. But suppose you have completed one project and wish to start another one without having to sign off Westlaw and back on again. You may start a new project during a current session as follows:

1. Go to the File menu.

2. Click "New Project."

You can also click "New Project" on the main button toolbar to perform this function.

If the previous project has not been saved, you will be reminded to save it. The "New Project" dialog box will be displayed. Enter the new project number or client identifier into the box, and click "OK."

OPENING PREVIOUSLY CREATED
PROJECT FILES

The main button toolbar has a button called "Open Project." Clicking on this button will display a list of all previously created projects. Click on the one you wish to open. Alternatively, you can open existing projects from the File menu by clicking "Open Project" there.

PRINTING AND DOWNLOADING

Various methods are available for printing or copying to a diskette or other places. You may print documents on an attached printer, download it to disk, download it to an e-mail, download it to a fax machine, save it on Westlaw, send it to a stand-alone printer, or send it to Westprint for mailing. Note that all users may not have all of these options.

The following steps are required:

1. With the document on your page, click the right mouse button, and choose "Send to Destination" from the menu. Or you may click the "File" menu and choose "Send to Destination." A third method is to choose "Select a Destination" from the main button toolbar.

2. Select the destination from the list given.

3. Choose the options desired from the dialog box on your screen.

OTHER AVAILABLE FUNCTIONS

Note that all functions available using Westmate have not been discussed. Those that are the same as those used when you access Westlaw from the Internet are given in earlier chapters.

SIGNING OFF

To sign off Westmate, you must first sign off Westlaw, then exit from Westmate in the following manner:

1. Either choose "Sign off Westlaw" from your File menu, or click the button for "Sign off Westlaw" on the main button toolbar.

2. Choose "Exit" from the Westmate file menu.

CONCLUSION

The Westlaw system has many additional functions that have not been described here. Detailed training manuals and database directories accompany subscriptions to the Westlaw service. Help is also available by contacting Customer Support or the West Group Reference Attorneys. Training is provided to subscribers in person or by telephone from a West Group Training representative.

ANSWERS TO REVIEW QUESTIONS

CHAPTER 1

1. *Primary sources*—binding authority, including laws, case decisions, administrative regulations, and other similar sources of law. *Secondary sources*—persuasive authority, including legal comments, annotations, articles in legal periodicals or law reviews, and legal encyclopedias.

2. You can gain access via the Internet or by using Westmate software.

3. The easiest method of accessing Westlaw is through your Internet browser via the World Wide Web by using the Westlaw home page (**http://www.westlaw.com**). You must first obtain an account from West, along with a password. You can then go to the Web page, key in your account number and password, and you will be online with Westlaw.

    In the alternative, you may obtain an account that includes Westmate software and then connect to the database directly via your modem. You will need to load the software onto your computer and make use of special commands.

CHAPTER 2

1. a. In the "Go to" section of the page, key in the following address:

    http://www.westlaw.com

    and hit "enter."

    b. Go to the "Sign on to westlaw.com" dialog box.

    c. Type in your Westlaw password in the "Password" box and your Client Identifier in the "Client ID" box.

    d. Click the "Sign on" button.

2. *Advantages*—convenience and ease of use; don't have to remember the password. *Disadvantages*—anyone using your Web browser can sign onto Westlaw with your saved password.

3. This feature enables your password to be encrypted as it is sent through the Internet.

4. **http://lawschool.westlaw.com**

CHAPTER 3   1. *Miller v. California,* 413 U.S. 15 (1973).

2. *Marvin v. Marvin.*

3. This will vary by state.

4. This will vary by state.

5. This issue will vary but should include all of the following: Can an owner of real property transfer ownership and still maintain a homestead on the property?

6. Type it in quotation marks, thus: "res ipsa loquitur".

7. Asterisks are used to take the place of a variable character.

8. a. A space between words means that at least one of the terms must appear.

   b. & retrieves documents containing two or more of the search terms.

   c. /s retrieves terms appearing in the same sentence.

   d. /p retrieves terms appearing in the same paragraph.

   e. /n retrieves terms appearing within a certain number of words.

   f. " " means the term in the quotation marks must appear exactly as it appears.

   g. % means the term following % should be excluded from the search.

9. XX-CORP (XX represents the two-letter postal abbreviation)

CHAPTER 4   1. You may print the current document, selected documents, all documents, or a list of citations.

2. Stand-alone printer, fax machine, e-mail, or download.

3. Word, WordPerfect for Windows, and PDF (with Adobe Acrobat Reader).

4. Printer to which print requests are delivered, e-mail address, and fax machine number.

5. **pr<enter>**

6. **L#**

7. You may enter several commands at the same time to avoid going from screen to screen when this effort is not required. Commands are separated by semicolons.

CHAPTER 5

1. Editorial enhancements are available including a summary of the case, headnotes and topics covered in the case, and key numbers that enable you to find cases with headnotes.

2. To obtain a review of the facts of several cases in order to choose those that apply to your case, use a synopsis field search. This search is accomplished by going to the Terms & Connectors search page, noting the box for "Field Restrictions," selecting "synopsis sy" from the drop-down list, typing your search terms, and clicking "Go."

3. It is used when your terms have common words or multiple meanings and enables you to limit your search to the law in the digest. In Terms & Connectors, click "Field Restrictions," and select "Digest DI" from the drop-down list. Type your search term, and click "Go."

4. **(di)**

5. West assigns topics and key numbers to all cases reported in its national reporter system. By means of these topics and key numbers, you can use West's publications and Westlaw together to find material. You can restrict your search to West Digest topics or key numbers by following these directions:

   a. Go to the Terms & Connectors search page.

   b. Click "Field Restrictions."

   c. Find the dialog box, and select "Topic to" from the drop-down list.

   d. Type your search terms in parentheses.

   e. Click "Go."

   Alternatively, you can type **"to"** after your initial search terms in the Terms & Connectors box. If you wish to use a key number instead of a digest topic, use the number after the **"to."** For example, you might used either **"to(134)"** or **"to(divorce)"** to find cases with headnotes for Topic 134, Divorce. If you wish to find cases on two different topics, type both key numbers in the parentheses. This search method is valuable for finding cases that discuss a certain specialty area of the law.

6. The Table of Authorities Service enables you to find all other cases that have been cited by your case. It is a useful tool for determining if there are hidden weaknesses in the case you are using, because it lists all cases on which your case relied. It also shows any significant negative history of those cases.

CHAPTER 6
1. Use "Scope" for basic information for research into statutes as well as descriptions of the database.

2. a. Find the drop-down list at the top of the page.

   b. Click "Find a Document" from the list.

   c. Click "Go."

   d. Type in the appropriate code for the statute being sought.

3. Go to the "Enter a Citation" text box, type **"fl st s 222.11,"** and click "Go."

4. Do a descriptive word search with either the Terms & Connectors or Natural Language method.

5. Use it when you wish to view a particular statute and the statutes that surround it.

6. Go to the drop-down list and select "Table of Contents Service;" click "Go."

7. Type the abbreviation for the statute, and click "Go."

8. Code of Federal Regulations, United States Code Annotated, Uniform Laws Annotated, State statutes, court rules, and administrative regulations.

9. It shows that a statute has been either amended or repealed. Click the "Update" link, and it will take you to the new legislation.

CHAPTER 7
1. Textbooks, periodicals, journals, newspapers, and other general information

2. Specialty databases provide information by law specialty area

3. TP-ALL

4. Online *Westlaw Directory;* printed *Westlaw Database Directory*

5. From the top of the page, select "Find a document" from the drop-down list; click "Go." Type the citation for the article in the "Enter a Citation" box.

6. *Westlaw Bulletin for the United States Supreme Court* - WLB-SCT

7. Mergers, acquisitions, tender offers, proxies, prospectuses, leveraged buyouts, current filings with the SEC

8. *Wall Street Journal* database (WSJ)

CHAPTER 8

1. KeyCite is one of the most current, comprehensive citation updating systems that allows you to automatically monitor changes in cases and statutes in which you are interested by clicking your mouse.

2. It covers all federal and state cases in West's reporter systems, over 1 million unpublished cases, 600 law reviews, *American Jurisprudence 2d, Couch on Insurance, Law of Federal Taxation, Norton on Bankruptcy,* Rutter Group publications, Witkin's *California Law,* and *Federal Practice and Procedure.*

3. You may use the Westlaw pull-down menu, the graphic KC icon in the tool bar, a status flag from a case display, or click on "KeyCite this headnote" if you are in a case headnote.

4. *Red flags*—the case is no longer "good law" because it has been overruled, reversed, vacated, or abrogated. *Yellow flags*—the case has some negative history.

5. Click "Citations to the Case" in the left frame of the History of the Case display.

6. KeyCite Alert

CHAPTER 9

1. Windows 95 or higher, VGA or SVGA monitor, 486/25 or Pentium (with Pentium preferred), 12MB memory with Windows 95 or 20MB with Windows NT, mouse or pointing device, CD-ROM drive, 14,400 bps modem or higher.

2. Insert CD-ROM disk into your CD-ROM drive; click "Next;" continue to click "Next" unless you wish to customize an option; then click "Finish."

CHAPTER 10

1. a. Click "Start."

   b. Choose "Programs."

   c. Choose "West Applications."

   d. Choose "Westmate."

   e. You will see the dialog box for signing on Westlaw. Type your password and client ID into the boxes provided for that purpose.

   f. Select a dialing location from the drop-down list entitled "My Location" if you are using a local modem.

   g. Check the appropriate billing method, either hourly or transactional.

     h. Click "OK."

     i. The "Welcome to New Westlaw" screen will appear.

2. a. Find the File menu, and choose "Sign off Westlaw."

     b. Click the proper button if you wish to save the current project on which you are working.

     c. You will see the Westlaw Time Summary box that indicates how much time you have been online with Westlaw. You are not disconnected from the system at this point.

     d. Click "OK."

     e. To exit from Westmate, choose "Exit" from your File Menu.

3. Choose "Options" from the Tools menu. Choose "Fonts" to change text type, font, font size, and color of document text. Choose "File Locations" for changing the location for storage of your files in a different download folder.

CHAPTER 11

1. Icon on the button bar, pull-down menu bar, buttons on the left on Main Menu

2. *Research menu*—choose "Westlaw Directory." *Main Screen*—click "Westlaw Directory" button. *Welcome screen*—click "Choose a Database" button on left side.

3. Use the right mouse button to move between pages of a document, go to a list of documents found, edit your query, locate the point at which particular terms appear, send the document to printer, or update the document on the screen.

4. Each research session is stored in an electronic folder called a "project."

5. Go to the File menu and click "New Project."

6. Either choose "Sign off Westlaw" from your File menu or click the button for "Sign Off Westlaw" on your Main Button Bar; choose "Exit" from the Westmate file menu.

INDEX